Female Led Relationship

The Couple's Guide to Female Dominance
and
Male Submission

Marisa Rudder

Please contact Marisa Rudder with any questions. Email: femaleledrelationshipbook@gmail.com

All of Marisa Rudder's Bestselling Books are Available on Amazon:

Love & Obey, Real Men Worship Women, Oral Sex for Women, Cuckolding, Spanking, Chastity, Turning Point, Swinging, Mommy's in Charge, Queendom, Hotwife, Femdom, and *Submissive.*

Printed in the United States of America Publisher's Cataloging-in- Publication data

ISBN: 978-1-7361835-8-8

DEDICATION

I would like to sincerely thank everyone who has supported me throughout the unfolding of this incredible vision of the *Love & Obey* movement. To all those who purchased and read each one of my books and followed my social media for the last four years, I offer my eternal gratitude. You inspired me to push for more female empowerment, sexual freedom, and the betterment of relationships and marriage. I could not have accomplished all that I have without your encouragement and support.

Thank you all for inspiring me to keep pushing forward. I love you all and dedicate this book to you for faithfully following my guidance and taking time out of your busy lives to include me in your journey. You are all so wonderful and so kind. Thank you for believing in this cause, which has already changed hundreds of thousands of lives.

My goal is to continue to fight for change and promote female led life globally. Men and women deserve to be happy in their lives and in their relationships and marriages. The future is female led, and the *Love & Obey* Movement is a safe space for all supportive men who worship their Queens and for couples who want to build successful Female Led Relationships and female led marriages.

You can find out more about the *Love & Obey* Female Led Movement and all my books on my website: http://www.loveandobey.com

Or follow me on social media:

FACEBOOK

https://www.facebook.com/femaleledrelationships

TWITTER

https://twitter.com/loveandobeybook

INSTAGRAM

https://www.instagram.com/femaleledrelationships

YOUTUBE

https://www.youtube.com/chan-nel/UCkX3wmd934WR103hStbzbiQ?view_as=subscriber

INTRODUCTION

Thousands of couples around the world are experiencing a revolution in their relationships by embracing a lifestyle called Female Led Relationship (FLR), in which the women are in charge. Increasing numbers of couples are discovering the thrill, intimacy, and joy that can only be found in a FLR. The future of the world is in the hands of smart, driven women who have emerged as the new dominant gender. This is a transitional period when women are gaining power and men are learning to be submissive to the loving authority of women.

In a Female Led Relationship, the woman is the leader and the man is the submissive. She has more power than the man does and has the final say on major issues. In a Female Led Relationship, the woman takes the reins and the man is happy to follow her lead as a supportive gentleman. Hence the rise of female dominance and male submission.

Since the 50s, there has been a change in every field, except relationships. It's no surprise that the divorce rate is already at 50 percent, and we're still trying to live by the rules that were made for marriages and relationships decades ago. Dating back to the turn of the century, men have traditionally been the breadwinners and leaders of the family, while women have stayed at home to raise children and care for the home. This was done to condition people to believe that men are superior and women are inferior. Since this is the case, the man should take charge. Where does that leave us, exactly? There is an increase in all of these negative trends, as well as many others: violence, divorce, the threat of war, natural disasters, the decline of traditional family values, an increase in violence against women, and a general trend toward greater inequality.

For many years, patriarchal conditioning ensured that women would be expected to play the submissive role that had been established for them. The Queen has always been the most vital part of the family because she is the one who gives birth. Thus, a woman is elevated above a man when she is in charge of something fundamental to survival. Regardless of her upbringing, that alone makes her superior. For example, in prehistoric times, men assumed their proper roles as servants to their women by providing for them through hunting and gathering. However, the truth that men are wired to serve women and the Queen makes the best leader in a relationship remains unaffected by centuries of patriarchal conditioning. Thus, the partnership is headed by the woman.

When men first began to dominate while women were to submit to them is a facet of life that has baffled scholars for a long time. It is believed that the church and legislation passed rules to restrict women's access to property and were major contributors to this patriarchal conditioning. The widespread belief that women should be subservient to men and the denial of basic rights like voting, property ownership, and leadership positions in the workplace played significant roles in maintaining this status quo. However, evidence suggests that in centuries prior, as well as in many cultures, the existence of female statues and deities shows women were worshipped and believed to possess great power as the givers and nurturers of life until men tried to suppress their power through patriarchy.

Today, the tides are turning. A modern woman is not only empowered to make decisions about her own life, career, and home but also to do so within the context of her marriage or other committed relationship. More and more women are assuming positions of power around the world, including in politics, business, and the home. It's safe to assume that this book will spark heated debate because it challenges accepted norms in contemporary culture. Even though female leadership is met with skepticism, it is on the rise. Female Led Relationships are reshaping marriage and the dating scene for the better, even though many people prefer business as usual and to continue with vanilla relationships based on rules developed more than 50 or 60 years ago.

In this book, I've compiled my findings from years of studying and living the Female Led Relationship lifestyle. This book builds on the ideas and experiences of my thousands of followers, and it is the natural sequel to my first book, *Love & Obey*. Here, I will explore the topics of what a Female Led Relationship means and how it is different from a male-led relationship. Also, this book will answer all your questions about FLR: how it works, its benefits, and how to establish this lifestyle. You'll learn everything you need to know to create and live a successful Female Led Relationship. How you treat your Queen on a daily basis will change as a result, because elevating her to the position of leader in your life and relationship requires you to give her the confidence and strength to do so. Once you commit to a relationship where the woman is in charge, you will find a new sense of meaning and purpose in life.

Are Female Led Relationships becoming more common? Absolutely. There has been a rise in FLR, which has been linked to increased levels of joy, excitement, and sexual satisfaction. Women are now at the helm of nations, governments, corporations, and even romantic partnerships. Kamala Harris made history in 2021 by becoming the first female Vice President of the United States. Sarah Thomas is the first female referee to work the Super Bowl, and Kim Ng became the first female general manager to be hired in Major League Baseball. The Olympic Games were dominated by women, who made up nearly half of all competitors. Once surfing was officially recognized as an Olympic sport, a female American athlete won the first ever surfing gold medal. Jeff Bezos, Amazon's founder, took a woman who was one of the first female astronauts with him on his first space flight.

A lot more women have succeeded in fields traditionally held by men. Years ago, as an engineering student, I faced the difficulty of breaking into a field that was traditionally dominated by men. Today, as the founder of the *Love & Obey* Movement, I have not only participated in but also witnessed the rise of female empowerment, which shows no signs of slowing down. It's time for women to step up and be leaders in the home and the bedroom. This shift is popular among men because it gives them an opportunity to be the kind, helpful partners society needs them to be.

Leopold von Sacher-Masoch was the first to say, "Man is the one who desires, woman the one who is desired." Simply put, this is the woman's one and only significant advantage. The leader of the Queen's army has been a respected figure for centuries, and he continues to serve at the pleasure of the monarch. Queen Elizabeth and Catherine the Great show that wars have been fought and won with women in command. What is it that's so powerful and mesmerizing as an alpha woman who projects the confidence and poise of a Queen? How is she able to reduce even the strongest man to a state of complete submission? Has the sexual revolution left men so far behind that they are unable to cope with the rise of female dominance and would just rather submit and serve their Queen? The fact is that men need relationships and women are the sources of power. So it's only a natural evolution for women to take the lead in relationships just as they have in leading countries, governments, corporations, and households.

What you'll notice in a relationship where the Queen is in charge is a dramatic increase in both love and passion. When women are given the opportunity to lead in a FLR, they undergo profound changes. Because of the transformation you've brought about in her, women regularly experience feelings of joy, inspiration, and love; in return, you experience feelings of acceptance, value, and specialness. Here is your chance to show her how much you truly respect and honor her as your Queen. There is nothing better than a strong woman who is allowed to be the Queen. As a result, you'll both be in a better place emotionally and spiritually.

Historically prevalent among the affluent, Female Led Relationships are on the rise in the public eye among today's elites, such as actors, athletes, and business executives. Why? For the simple reason that strong men appreciate a strong Queen. When there is a strong, powerful Queen and an even stronger King who recognizes her worth and gives her the reins, the kingdom is unstoppable. What we have here is the foundation for a relationship in which the woman takes the lead. The man is not feeble or unimportant. He's the one who holds everything together; he's the general. Now more than ever, women are the ones behind the wheel. I can think of numerous real-world examples of women who took control of their lives and careers and thereby transformed the lives of men.

Many couples are discovering that magical things can happen when the Queen takes the lead in their relationship. You begin to think and act differently toward one another. The woman becomes a Queen, and her divine nature shines through. The man transforms into the type of gentleman who sees his role as purely utilitarian. The welfare and desires of his Queen are his primary concern, hence he welcomes the opportunity to experience true male submission.

Join us on this journey of passion, which could turn your marriage and relationship from humdrum to thrilling. You and your Queen have earned the chance to take your journey to the next exciting level of romance and adventure. Create the Female Led Relationship of your dreams.

TABLE OF CONTENTS

CHAPTER 1
What Is a Female Led Relationship?

A Female Led Relationship is one where the woman takes the lead and assumes the role of the dominant partner, with men taking on the more submissive role. The woman will be in charge of the important decisions and carries more authority in the relationship. There are several reasons why couples decide to get into a Female Led Relationship, and many more are switching from normal marriages and relationships to wife led marriages. I receive thousands of messages from couples making the transition and from men actively seeking a dominant woman. Female led lifestyle is beginning to emerge in media, such as movies and TV shows, with so many great female characters taking charge.

Some of the classics are even changing their formula from male-dominated to female. The very popular James Bond series is a great example of the move from the Agent 007 being the strong, tough lead character to now females taking over for the 2021 release. Wonder Woman was a sensation as a follow-up to Superman, and she is the superior character in

1

Justice League. The show *The Equalizer* casts Queen Latifah instead of the usual male character played by Denzel Washington. With female led growing and the abundance of strong, capable female characters depicted in mainstream media, more men are craving female authority.

There are only three things you need to be concerned with in life—your relationship with your partner or spouse, your relationship with yourself, and your relationship with God. FLR has the power to transform your life because you and your Queen are on a journey of exploration together. Female led life turns the focus inward so that you and your Queen are facilitating your growth through your experiences together. You also learn by developing the necessary skills like integrity, moral values, honesty, open communication, intimacy, empathy, forgiveness, and compersion.

Female Led Relationships are a proven winning formula for an exciting sex life, a deeper bond, and everlasting happiness. How you choose to spend each day will determine the course of your life. Do you choose boredom and jealousy? Or do you prefer honesty, respect, admiration, inspiration, and a feeling of ecstasy and adventure in exploring all that life has to offer? If so, Female Led Relationship is for you.

Of course, there will be challenges with FLR, such as deciding who will manage the money, make household decisions, and plan social events. Understanding the guidelines of how to exist in this type of relationship is crucial. There will always be issues to overcome, but generally, there will be fewer power struggles when the leader, the Queen, is established right from the start, with the man being the supportive gentleman. A great example of female led is the Queen, head of the British Royal Family. The Queen is the leader, and Prince Philip was her supportive gentleman, a role he fulfilled dutifully till his passing. Prince Philip was a wonderful example of how an alpha male could still be alpha but also accept his role as submissive to his Queen. Many may say it's just tradition, but Prince Philip has said on many occasions that he had to adjust to the role and complete a lot of training to be able to succeed.

The same is true for couples in Female Led Relationships. The misconception is that men who agree to be in this type of relationship are naturally submissive or weak. This could not be further from the truth. Some men are submissive and enjoy being with a stronger woman, but many alpha men are just as eager to serve a powerful woman as their Queen, and they are happy to be the supportive gentleman. Even in patriarchal times, the only person who could control a man was a woman. There are many examples of how powerful men were brought to their knees, good or bad, by women. Wallace Simpson changed the course of history when King Edward abdicated the throne. King Henry VIII, a notorious womanizer, made his mistress Anne Boleyn a queen and went against the church to do it — for a woman. There are even modern-day examples, like Bill Clinton's impeachment due to a woman and Prince Harry marrying a bi-racial common American woman, Megan Markle, and moving away from the monarchy to live their lives in North America — all under a woman's influence.

Women are powerful in many areas, and in the Female Led Relationship, you are submitting to that power. You show your ultimate respect in the bedroom, which was once an area of male dominance, and now becomes a place of female worship. So why does this work so effortlessly? Women have become accustomed to taking charge. In *Gone with the Wind,* I was fascinated when the men went off to war and the women still continued to survive and took charge. In a world where women were expected to follow men, in their absence, females stepped up and managed everything.

Women have a natural ability to lead because they are multi-taskers and great communicators. Women form relationships with other people better than men. They are collaborators, and nothing can get done as an island. Today in 2021, women are finally exercising their natural ability to be the ruler and men as the supporter. Oral sex is part of the supportive man's duties, and in Female Led Relationships, sex is for the Queen's pleasure. How you pleasure your Queen becomes your opportunity to show how much you adore her. Your willingness to ensure her happiness will transform your life's purpose. When men discover their new life purpose of loving, obeying, and serving a superior female, they will find peace and contentment. In addition, the loving female authority will provide him with tremendous amounts of love and affection.

The general rule implies that when you decide to create a Female Led Relationship, you must both agree that she is in charge. This is of great importance to establish early on to prevent any power struggles later on. There may be additional challenges with men who like the idea of being in a Female Led Relationship but are unable to fully commit due to previous patriarchal conditioning. My seven books in the *Love & Obey* series help with this transition properly into the lifestyle. It is my hope that this book, which serves as the ultimate guide to everything female led, will help you to create the perfect Female Led Relationship or female led marriage for you and your Queen. One that will not only be based on the foundation of honesty, trust, and open communication but one that will allow both of you to thrive and be fully satisfied every day of your life.

Women seem to come alive when there are fewer arguments and more constructive support happening in daily life. When you listen to her intently, participate in conversations, and encourage her ideas and goals, you help your Queen become a dynamic, successful person who is inspirational to everyone around you, including your kids. Children mimic their parents, and they need examples of success, maturity, and love to inspire them daily. A woman with a strong supportive man is free to be the shining star she is meant to be, and it leads me to think about the saying, "Behind every great woman is a great man." So, obedience to a woman should never be seen as weakness. Strong men know the tremendous benefits of supporting a strong woman.

Women have felt their power growing each year. For many, "The Future is Female" and "Girl Boss" is the new normal. I began to notice this sharp increase in female empowerment themes in movies, TV shows, YouTube, governments, corporations, and households. Everywhere, I have witnessed examples of women taking charge, and now it is becoming a worldwide phenomenon in relationships and society. They embrace the idea of female superiority and leadership.

The support I received from men about reading *Love & Obey* and practicing it daily, and the hundreds of testimonials I received, was overwhelming. Men everywhere tell me how they enjoy and have learned to worship women. Empowering a woman to lead should not be viewed as negative, as it helps to build a stronger, fulfilling relationship. Women are enjoying and welcoming the new role to teach men how to become loving and obedient. I believe that this is the best lifestyle for a truly successful and happy relationship and offers the most opportunity for both people to grow and evolve together.

What needs to change in our society? About 70 percent of health and social workers are women which means they are caregivers even in their work lives. This makes home life even more stressful and women are often overworked, underpaid, and unhappy. There is still an increase in violence against women, and in the developing world, girls are forced to prepare for marriage and still must fight for the same right to education as boys. A startling 496 million women around the world are illiterate. Women are still given a disproportionate share of the household chores and responsibilities — tasks like walking miles for water and caring for younger siblings.

Approximately 41,000 girls under the age of 18 each day are forced to get married. Without access to adequate family planning, contraception or health care, they get pregnant early. Women still earn less than men even though in most cultures they are responsible for taking care of elderly parents as well as the family. About one-third of married women in the developing world have no control over major household purchases, placing them in a position of less power than their men.

Female Led Relationships and female led marriages are growing and more couples are eager to explore and create lifestyles conducive to experiencing the best version of dominance and submission, allowing the Queen to step into her position as supreme leader and you, her man to be her submissive supportive gentleman.

CHAPTER 2
Do Female Led Relationships Work?

Female Led Relationships are vastly different from normal relationships which tend to be male led and based on patriarchy. So do Female Led Relationships work? The answer is yes, they absolutely do. There is no relationship or marriage which offers more fulfillment and happiness for both people, and this is confirmed by the thousands of couples who have reported that their lives, relationships, and marriages have been dramatically transformed and saved by creating a Female Led Relationship. All of the Queen's needs are met and there is a loving, obedient man who puts her on a pedestal and worships her every day.

I have found that women love Female Led Relationships because they can finally be free to assert their dominance and can step into their rightful role as leaders. Women have always naturally led households and made decisions at home, and this is where it all begins. A properly run household makes a happy, successful family. Children learn most from their homes, and what happens in our homes and family relationships affects us over our lifetime.

I can recall the number of times in early relationships when I purposely suppressed my dominant, take-charge personality for the sake of my partner. In the beginning, many strong women felt they had to abide by society's patriarchal rules allowing their men to have control while they maneuvered from being second. However, this eventually causes problems because a female led woman cannot suppress her nature forever. As I have experienced, at some point, the Queen will be unhappy being submissive when her true nature is to be a leader. Having control over their relationship, household, kids, finances, and everything else, is just a part of a woman's personality.

The freedom to lead in relationships allows women to be involved in their rightful role as Queen and prevents her from feeling suppressed. These are some reasons as to why Female Led Relationships work. Female Led Relationships defy the traditional relationship dynamic in which the man has authority over the woman. They also defy traditional gender roles that our patriarchal society has imposed on women, and it gives women a chance to make meaningful decisions, changes, and contributions to their household without having to go through a male's approval first. There is less of a power struggle in a Female Led Relationship, as the roles are clear. Knowing she has her partner's support, the woman can make her decisions peacefully. While it is a debated issue, some women feel that an FLR allows them more control of their partner and allows them to change bad habits and help them better themselves.

The advantage of a Female Led Relationship is that it sets clear roles and removes the potential for power struggles. It establishes the proper hierarchy. No one in British Royalty questions who is at the head. The Queen reigns supreme, and everyone in the UK and worldwide show their respect to her. There is a wonderful scene where Churchill visited Queen Elizabeth for the first time, and he was standing while conversing with her for an hour. The Queen was perplexed but later Churchill explained that it was his duty to show respect to her by remaining standing until she allowed him to sit. He wasn't allowed to interrupt her or speak before she spoke. These rules help to establish order, and having clear roles in the relationship reduces fights.

Both you and your Queen must be familiar with the rules as they will need to be reinforced constantly, especially in the beginning. As human beings, we tend to fall back into learned behavior, and you will want to act out and maybe speak out of turn to your Queen. You may yell and raise your voice inappropriately, and all of these behaviors must change if the relationship is to run smoothly. My suggestion is to write out the rules and have them be visible to deter arguments.

In a Female Led Relationship, a woman is set free. She is free to make decisions about her desires and yours. She is no longer controlled by a man, and by allowing herself to experience her Goddess power, she furthers her evolution. The Female Led Relationship is here to stay, and women are no longer tolerating abuse, control, and bad behavior of men. Even in good relationships, a woman can be made to feel controlled and left sexually unfulfilled. The mere idea of sex for a man's orgasm and pleasure is one of the main reasons women are changing.

While power struggles within relationships are common, if a Queen finds herself with less power in a relationship, researchers found it takes a much greater emotional toll on her. Inequality within a relationship doesn't cost men as much because they are still cushioned by a broader system of male privilege. Men may rule the world but women rule the roost. Women wield considerably more decision-making power than men within marriages. Research suggests that a marker of a healthy marriage is men accepting influence from their wives. Researchers found that wives, on average, displayed more power than their husbands during problem-solving discussions, regardless of who brought up the topic of discussion.

What works for a man does not work for a woman, and as more research is done into women's biology, physiology, and psychology the more we realize that change is not only imminent but necessary. Patriarchy is over, and the Female Led Relationship will usher in a new era, one where women will take charge and men will be the supportive gentleman. This new role for men should never be viewed as weakness as there is great responsibility in being the supporter. I have always believed that women were meant to lead. They are more suited to lead as they are armed with better communication styles, flexibility, empathy, and intuition.

Patriarchy dictated in biblical stories that in the story of Adam and Eve, Adam disobeyed God and took the apple from Eve, his wife. This is how it was taught to me. But as far back as when I was a child in Catholic schools, I felt that we could interpret this story as Adam obeyed his wife Eve and did what she wanted, even at the risk of disobeying God, classic FLR. Since the dawn of time, men have served women.

Why did men go out and hunt and do the manual work? Because each day, their duty was to provide service for their women who remained home, managed the household, and took care of the children.

The strength of the home and the household is one of the most important tasks and provides a foundation for people to operate. Women were leaders in ensuring that everything in the home was taken care of. Only in the case of attempting to control women and suppress their power was being at home considered a weakness. The conditioning from patriarchy kept women down for decades, but now everything is changing.

In the past, the world was run by men, but male authoritative relationships are not as effective. They don't work. The divorce rate is hovering around 50 percent. This is the result of dominant male relationships in the last 50 to 100 years. It is interesting to note that because of the breakdown in the household, with more households run by single moms, the world evolved to be female led. Male leadership only leads to conflict, arguments, and growing apart. Wars are a male idea. Fighting, in general, is a male idea. Rarely do you see two women getting into a physical altercation. Women in same-sex couples are rarely reported for domestic abuse. Why? Because it is part of the male led paradigm. When women feel ignored and pressured by men, they generally start spending more time with friends who make them feel appreciated and allow open communication.

Many women feel they must suppress a feeling of superiority for fear of upsetting their man's fragile ego. This leads to women feeling underappreciated and stifled. Eventually, a woman hiding the need to feel her power becomes depressed, disgruntled, and angry. Men, you don't want to be in a relationship with an angry woman. My simple advice is to be obedient to your woman. Even if you have not always obeyed in the past, you must obey her now. Allow yourself to be directed by the commands of your woman. When a woman sees you respect her for good choices and intelligent decisions, she will change her conduct and be pleased by your behavior. Then, you will be rewarded. When you reward a woman like a Queen, she will rise to embody a Queen, which means more happiness as you will be proud to be at her side, serving her.

When women are treated like Queens, they will take on the role in their appearance, behavior, and outlook, which will inspire you to be more of a gentleman. You will worship your woman's intelligence, heart, and beauty. Your woman will take command of your heart as you submit to her, and she will guide you wisely by the imperishable beauty of her gentle and loving authority over you, which is very precious. Simone de Beauvoir, the author of *The Second Sex*, is credited with spearheading the women's movement. Her writing explained why it was difficult for talented women to become successful. The obstacles de Beauvoir cites include women's inability to make as much money as men do in the same profession, women's domestic responsibilities, society's lack of support toward talented women, and women's fear that success will lead to an annoyed husband or prevent them from even finding a husband at all.

She also argues that women lack ambition because of how they are raised, noting that girls are told to follow the duties of their mothers, whereas boys are told to exceed the accomplishments of their fathers. Along with other influences, Simone de Beauvoir's work helped the feminist movement to erupt, causing the formation of le Mouvement de Libération des Femmes or the Women's Liberation Movement. Contributors to the Women's Liberation Movement include Simone de Beauvoir, Christiane Rochefort, Christine Delphy, and Anne Tristan. Through this movement, women gained equal rights such as the right to an education, a right to work, and a right to vote.

There are many other reasons why an FLR is so appealing to women. If we look at some of the attributes important to women, like finding an empathetic, understanding man who is a good listener. Women love to communicate and talk, so they desire a thoughtful listener, which men must practice and work on regularly. Men who are in Female Led Relationships or desire to be in one will tend to be more in touch with their deeper emotional side, and therefore, are accustomed to women who communicate well. They tend to develop these skills, which strong, dominant women desire. Men who are good listeners are present and attentive, not just waiting until it's their turn to talk, and they are able to follow the rhythm of a good discussion and adapt to it. Couples who don't learn to consciously communicate will face issues in intimacy, conflict, and relational growth. Understanding your Queen's inner world and having them understand yours is pivotal to true connection, and most women desire this connection in a Female Led Relationship.

Lastly, a plethora of evidence reveals that females are superior to men in many ways. Science proves this with the findings of an extra X in every female cell, far from being redundant, is instrumental in ensuring that women have a distinct genetic advantage. Humans have 23 chromosome pairs. One of those pairs consists of our two sex chromosomes. Females have two X chromosomes (XX), males have one X and one Y (XY). The X chromosome has about 1,000 genes; the Y has maybe 70. The X is one of the biggest chromosomes and contains extremely significant genes, which makes and maintains the brain. Why would nature bestow this extra dose of chromosome the more important one to women if were they not to be superior? We don't need nature to confirm the answer to this, just one look at all of the accomplishments of women against all obstacles and it is evident. Hence, in a Female Led Relationship, women are taking their rightful place as leaders.

CHAPTER 3
Why Do Men Like Female Led Relationships?

What is surprising is that men tend to initiate the exploration and transition into Female Led Relationships. A large percentage of men desire female led marriages even more than women in the beginning. So why do men like Female Led Relationships? After helping thousands of couples, and specifically men with their marriages and finding suitable partners, I believe that men are indeed inspired by strong capable women, ultimately desiring a woman they can treat like a Queen. Men are looking for a woman who captures them, excites them, and someone they can be proud of.

Research shows that two-thirds of men fall in love with a woman very similar to their mother, so men will be attracted to women who have similar qualities to their mothers, as this is the person they tend to love and respect the most. Relationship expert Rachel Lloyd says, "It's well known that we tend to migrate toward people who share similar traits with us and, to varying degrees, we seek to recreate aspects of our original relationships with our parents." Our earliest relationships, especially with our mother, influence how we can connect as adults in romantic and other contexts and also create internalized scripts or working models of how relationships work.

Other factors may be driving the need for a strong woman. Today, men are under a tremendous amount of stress and anxiety about relationships, love, and life, and it's even more difficult having to find their place in a world where women are dominating. They must resolve their issues with patriarchal conditioning from childhood and how they think they're supposed to be as a modern man existing in this new world. Since men are still expected to take on leadership positions in their working life, they are happy to take less of this role in their personal life.

Therefore, Female Led Relationships take the stress of a leadership role off of men who would prefer not to have the pressure. It releases them from a role of authority that they might otherwise have been pressured to take at home and at work. Some men would prefer to adopt the gentler role in a relationship, such as looking after children, tending to the home, cooking and cleaning, and earning less income without the stress of being the breadwinner.

Men in Female Led Relationships are looking for strong women who can consistently keep them in line and take control. Consistency makes a man form good habits and he feels he has been justly disciplined when he is spanked for misbehavior or disobedience. He understands that discipline and punishment is part of a consistent and fair system of FLR rules and consequences.

Men love Female Led Relationships because they can appreciate their partner more and better recognize their worth. They see their partners as equals, rather than as below them. A Female Led Relationship also helps a man learn to serve and worship his woman better as he gains more of an understanding of what turns women on and how to communicate better. They have the opportunity to evolve in an FLR with the help of their Queen. Men are attracted to strong, confident women because they are proud to serve a Queen, not a maid, and they are addicted to the chase. A strong woman represents the trophy. Sure, he likes to be mothered and taken care of from time to time, but men need unpredictability and excitement. That's where a strong woman comes in, and in a Female Led Relationship, men desire to serve.

Let's face it, confident women are winners in the boardroom and the bedroom, so confidence is sexy and a real turn-on. Strong women know how to please their men in bed and demand what they want, and this is just too irresistible to pass up. Think Sharon Stone in the movie *Basic Instinct* or Mila Jovovich in the movie *Resident Evil*. What man can resist a real temptress?

The alpha woman is looking for an absolutely independent man, both financially and psychologically. He must have a healthy ego and his own opinion, hobbies, and friends. An alpha woman is looking for an equal partner, someone to walk with, not behind or in front of. One thing that men will appreciate in a strong woman is her deep appreciation for her freedom, and she truly appreciates a man who respects that. Women can't stand being restricted in any way. Men love their freedom too, so this can be a win-win situation once you ensure there is adequate time spent together and intimately.

Strong women want to be challenged. They want to compete with their partner intellectually, physically, and emotionally. Men will be often kept on their toes at all times, and it's almost impossible to ignore or dismiss a powerful woman who also likes to push herself, is ambitious, successful, and capable. These are all qualities admired in other men, so they are often thrilled when they find these very qualities in a woman they are attracted to.

Today, couples are searching for ways to keep their relationship and interaction intense, intimate, and exciting. Female Led Relationships and female led marriages offer more ways to keep life interesting with several additional areas to explore. Maybe your Queen desires cuckolding, or maybe you both want to add the element of domination and submission with spanking, BDSM, and role-playing. Maybe you prefer the freedom of consensual non-monogamy where you can be in a committed relationship and have the freedom to explore additional partners.

The best activities for couples in successful relationships and marriages are those that are done together. Some questions you can ask yourself to determine the appropriate activities are: Can it be done regularly? Do you both enjoy it? Can you communicate properly? What's great about Female Led Relationships is that you and your Queen can explore together and there are endless ways to switch things up. Men love the variety as well. Men crave a woman who is naturally mysterious and exciting. That's what keeps the spice alive.

Too often, couples get into a rut that they cannot get out of because the source of regular relationships is the outdated paradigm of patriarchy. Most women, if they are honest, do not want to be a slave to a man. She's not going to choose giving her man a blow job or having intercourse for 5 to 10 minutes, then having everything done once he cums over her own pleasure and desires. Too often women who are stuck in regular relationships are unhappy at the core because they remain unsatisfied. Men can sense when the Queen is angry and unfulfilled and places even more strain on the relationship.

Generally, women tend to be more in touch with the fear, pain, depression, and loss they feel in their present relationships, which tie into the past. Whereas men tend to be more in touch with their anger. Men don't get a lot of sympathy or empathy when they come across as angry or demanding, but often their anger is a cover for the hurt and the fear that they feel.

In an FLR, both you and the Queen are focused on each other's needs every day. The tendency to grow apart and become bored is rare because the focus is inward. You place her on a pedestal and learn to worship her properly, and she, in turn, rewards you with more excitement, good regular sex, and a general sense of positivity and happiness. Men desire a purring kitty over a vicious lioness any day.

CHAPTER 4
Levels of a Female Led Relationship

All relationships and marriages are not equal and even Female Led Relationships can take on different forms. Love is amazing. But love is also complicated and confusing. Relationships are challenging and rarely straightforward. How do we make the best of the love in our lives, especially as it pertains to romantic relationships? By learning and working to be the best partners we can be. In a Female Led Relationship success happens when there are rules, guidelines, and boundaries have been established. This means every relationship or marriage will be different and will have different levels of control. No matter what happens, the foundation of a Female Led Relationship is that the woman is in charge.

Here are the different levels of control in a Female Led Relationship:

Level One

The lowest level of an FLR woman involves having a limited amount of control and taking the lead on some decisions, but not all. Her dominance could also spill over into the bedroom, which can make for a more exciting sex life. In general, at the lowest level, couples will be starting out on their FLR journey. Typically, the man will show his service to the Queen by allowing her to take control of daily activities, outings, kids' schedules, and TV viewing. This is a great way to begin your female led journey and helps your Queen to become accustomed to taking the lead. Consider this to be the springboard for moving on to other levels.

This is also a good time for men to learn how to adapt to their role as supportive gentlemen. You both can work out the complexities of adopting these new roles, and it can represent the turning point for going from a normal relationship to FLR. Though this light level is rarely depicted, it is an important entry point for most couples who want to build a successful long-term relationship.

Level Two

In the next level of a Female Led Relationship, the woman's role as the dominant partner begins to get a little more serious. She will start to call the shots on more areas of the relationship and dominate her man in the bedroom more too. The man may take on more traditionally "female" roles in the relationship, such as taking care of the household, handling the kids, and completing more chores.

At this level, your Queen will take responsibility for the daily schedules and have a written agenda of duties. She will generally control the finances and decide on activities, the delegation of household duties, and any other serious decisions to be made. She may also decide on how sex should progress and if as a couple you will begin to explore cuckolding, hotwifing, or any other ways to spice up the sex life.

This second level is great for couples who are happy with the beginning level and have done so for at least six months. Do not proceed to this level if there was major hesitation at the lowest level. At this point, you should be happy and excited to already be in a Female Led Relationship. Many couples remain at this point and are perfectly happier staying here.

Level Three

The third level of an FLR involves complete submission to the Queen's desires. It's her way or the highway. Men must learn to submit completely, and I recommend that you start your study with my book *Turning Point*, which will help you to address any past conditioning that might be holding you back. It is at this level that the Queen may introduce hotwifing, cuckolding, spanking, and some BDSM if she desires. She may want to direct all of your sexual activities.

Your duty to serve her every day will become extremely important. She may decide that chastity and orgasm control is necessary, and she may prohibit masturbation to ensure all of your focus is on her. You will treat her like a Queen at all times, never interrupt her, never raise your voice to her, and spend every moment ensuring she is pleased. She will also have the responsibility of assuming complete control and directing all activities, events, and happenings in the household. She may take over the finances.

Sex is for the Queen's pleasure, and you must ensure that your oral skills are perfected. You can refer to my book *Oral Sex for Women*, which you will get all the necessary instruction needed to properly pleasure your Queen. You must satisfy her needs before your own. Communication will be mandatory at this point because you will need to identify what her needs are and what changes must be made. You need to be communicating every step of the way.

Level Four

The most extreme level of a Female Led Relationship is where the Queen demands that her man be her servant. Most couples don't need to get to this level, but many love the extremes of it. The man can be sissified, and he can literally become the servant to his Queen. She may decide to place him in a cage or in a time-out corner, punish him, do spanking, bondage, and more. She may decide on cuckolding and having her Bull over while her man serves you both. There often is a formal contract created to outline the duties of her man to service the Queen.

Even though this level is extreme, there must still be full consent from both you and your Queen. You must analyze if you truly derive pleasure from being in servitude, locked up, and completely controlled sometimes in an inhumane way. Your Queen also must decide if this is what she wants. This extreme level is reserved for those couples who are fully on board with taking their FLR to an extreme level. The activities at this level are not mandatory. A reverse example of this was in the movie *Fifty Shades of Grey*. Christian required Anna to sign a contract and be at his beck and call at all times. She also had to experience spankings and many sessions in his private room.

Similarly, in the reverse, this is what happens in a Female Led Relationship at the extreme level. Safe words must be implemented and communication about boundaries become very important and must not be skipped. Some couples enjoy the formality of the Queen dressed in leather and latex, and you, the man dressed as a sissy or submissive clothing of her choice. She may decide what clothes you wear, where you go out, and if she wants you to be collared and pegged on a regular basis. The important thing to remember is that you both want to take your relationship to this level and there is a mutual agreement.

It is essential to understand the difference between being a dominatrix and a Queen. The *Love & Obey* version of the Female Led Relationship lies between level one and level three. Though I am aware that level four happens, a Female Led Relationship must function as a successful relationship or marriage first. In the event you are already in a successful FLR and want to add elements of Femdom, these are available to you.

BDSM, spanking, D/S, age play, sissification, chastity, and more are all considered more intense versions of loving FLR, but you and your Queen have the choice of exploring as little or as much or more intense activities as you wish. You must only understand that being in a Female Led Relationship does not mean your Queen needs to be a dominatrix. The media

25

loves to portray dominant women as cruel and inhumane, but this is neither conducive to building a successful marriage or interaction nor will it necessarily lead to long-term success. Female led should never be used as an opportunity for abuse. There must always be consent from both you and your Queen.

I always think back to the General Adaptation Syndrome (GAS) by Hans Selye, in which he says that an organism under stress can become stronger if the stressor is only intermittent. If the stressor is continual and prolonged, the organism eventually dies. I believe that the same is true for relationships — cruelty can only go so far before it becomes destructive. The aim of a woman taking control is not to be cruel, though it happens with dominatrixes and their clients. The difference is that a dominatrix gets paid to administer what the man wants in terms of cruelty, punishment, and discipline as part of his deep-seated desires. Because essentially, she is being paid to do what a man desires, which is not female led in my view.

So, it is not advisable for your Queen to become a dominatrix in order to be female led. If she wishes to insert some dominance and fun practices like light spanking, BDSM, dressing up in leather to spice up your fun, sexy times, then this is permissible. I discuss how to raise the intensity of the Female Led Relationship by adding in elements of spanking, punishment, relationship discipline, and more in my book *Femdom*. Light levels of a FLR can be more loving and involve you following your Queen's lead and allowing her to make the decisions and lead in the bedroom.

Female Led Relationships are more about what happens in daily life and your interactions. A Female Led Relationship is only successful if it is loving and both people can feel appreciated, loved, and respected in their roles. Your Queen will still be loving and sexual while she leads, and you can still be respectful and supportive while being submissive. There are many reasons why men and women choose a Female Led Relationship. In some instances, it's a simple case of an aggressive woman and a passive man falling into place naturally. In other cases, an alpha man recognizes the benefits that her leadership would bring to the relationship, and convinces, teaches, or reprograms her man to accept her loving female authority over him and gives him proper direction. These teachings have led me to understand the rules that men must observe to create the best Female Led Relationship.

If men understand these rules early on, women will experience less stress and anxiety with having to train or reprogram their men on how to behave and serve daily. If men follow the rules, the relationship will be generally positive, rewarding, and fulfilling.

CHAPTER 5
Types of Submissive Men

There are varying degrees of submission in Female Led Relationships and different types of submissive men. Which type of submissive style will you want to be for your Queen? When you set off down the path to explore this modern role of the submissive man, you will feel uncertain about how you should behave, what your relationship should entail, and how it all fits in with the way society is and should be.

We've all been taught that men should be manly and alpha, meet the woman of their dreams, take control of work and the household, and make all the decisions in life. Men should also neither cry nor become emotional.

However, all of this is based on faulty conditioning, which has been shown to be harmful and destructive to the growth of men. When it comes to being submissive, you need to feel free to explore any level of submission that works for you and your Queen. Here are the different levels of submission that you should explore and the types of submissive men.

Supportive Gentleman

A supportive gentleman is a man who behaves in a gentle and chivalrous way with women. Supportive gentlemen are often alpha men in society at large and possess the qualities of a traditional man, but their conduct conforms to a high standard of correct behavior, respect, obedience, and service to his Queen. A new term for this type of man is "male wife," which has been described as a man who chooses to be submissive to his wife, who is essentially the girl boss or the woman in charge.

Think of the supportive gentleman as being like a Knight in the Queendom. You are a man in service to Your Majesty. You worship, love, obey, and serve your Queen. You may dominate in society, but when it comes to your Queen, you are submissive. Supportive gentlemen often live in monogamous relationships with their Queens providing all the services they desire. The supportive gentleman is the lightest version of submission. Your Queen assumes all the power and leadership of the household and at work, but you take your direction from her, and in this regard, you are submissive in bed as well.

However, many couples practice FLR at home while they are free to live normal lives outside. So, as the supportive gentleman, you continue to be dominant and in charge at work. This works for people who are exploring Female Led Relationships. You may have decided that you are interested in being submissive and are adding aspects of FLR to your lives.

The supportive gentleman is the Queen's champion. You are there to be her strongest advocate and it is only through your servitude and desire to submit to her can she step into power as Queen. Supportive gentlemen can take charge at work and be leaders in their industries. They will enjoy the dual roles because they welcome the relief of having a strong woman to make the decisions at home. Generally, at this level, couples prefer to keep things light and will not engage in aspects of femdom, BDSM, discipline, and punishment. There still can be rules and agreements, but the interaction is much more that of the Queen, with a loyal knight or head of the army who is subordinate but goes out and fights for her and supports her.

I've always been very interested in the dynamic between Queens like Queen Elizabeth I and the strong men who were submissive to her yet helped lead her armies to many victories. I believe that she was one of the greatest Queens because she commanded this respect from men who supported her.

Submissive Man

A Submissive or Sub is a man who is still masculine but is free to explore his emotional and softer side. He is generally more agreeable and more adept at handling all sorts of tasks, including work, household duties, and childcare, while having great empathy, communication, and listening. The submissive man or sub has made a choice to willingly give up some or all of their male power and control and surrender to a dominant Queen. If you are submissive, you choose to allow your Queen to take control of you. This is the next level of submission, a more intense version than the supportive gentleman.

The submissive man can be submissive at work and outside the home. I was always very delighted when a man would show that he was submissive and treated me with respect in places like my work, the gym, and events. There is power in submission, and submissive men who show respect to women are in demand. As a submissive you have accepted your desire to surrender control to a superior female. You will generally be submissive at all times, when you are with your Queen at home and outside. Submissive men can have a dual role in bed where they are the Queen's primary partner, servicing her and ensuring she is sexually fulfilled, but they may also explore consensual non-monogamy with cuckolding and hotwifing where a third outside partner is involved.

The sub will generally be watching or not even be present during sexual interactions. You may explore chastity and be given the task of orally pleasuring your Queen at all times. Sex is for the Queen's pleasure is the first rule of Female Led Relationships, so it's important to understand that your sole purpose in your submissive role is to please your Queen. Consensual non-monogamy practices are not mandatory as part of submission. You and your Queen are free to explore D/S and any or all activities you wish.

Sissy

A Sissy is a man who idolizes women so much that he desires to be feminized. He wants to abandon all of his masculinity and become as feminine as he possibly can become. He likes to wear female lingerie, dress in female clothing, wear makeup, and behave in a totally feminine manner. Beyond the sub, he has made a choice to willingly give up all of his masculine qualities and surrender completely to his dominant Queen. Sissy training is a process where submissive men learn to take on traditionally female roles. The submissive, known as a sissy, learns to adopt ultra-feminine behaviors and perform feminine activities under the guidance of his dominant partner. Sissy training is usually performed as part of a BDSM role-playing scene or BDSM lifestyle.

After adopting a completely feminine persona, sissies are no longer considered men by their Queens and rarely perform any sexual acts with them. They are typically cuckolded regularly and humiliated for their lost manhood by their Queens. But sissies welcome the chance to explore and show their femininity freely. Many men begin with cross-dressing as their early experience being a sissy, then transition into the full role. Cross-dressing and shaving the body are other common elements of sissy training as they help transform the male body into one that appears more feminine.

Sissification or sissy training is the process whereby a submissive man emasculates himself and takes on personality traits or roles usually associated with women. He effectively becomes a caricature of what a woman is, based on societal stereotypes. This can include anything from wearing a dress and tights to soften body language, wearing lots of pink, or only responding to a feminine name. What takes place during sissy play depends entirely on the submissive partner's chosen sissy role.

For example: A 'Maid Sissy' cooks, cleans, and wants to take on domestic chores, whereas a 'Toddler Sissy' plays the role of a young female who can't do anything for herself. Some sissy play is a form of humiliation, while others concentrate more on the role reversal, age play, and gender-bending aspects of this role-play. Many sissies are assumed to be homosexual, but this is false. Sissies welcome the opportunity to be under the training of a powerful alpha woman or dominatrix. Many sissies enjoy the role so much they would rather be with women and have this type of influence and interaction. Women love it too because they share many aspects of femininity and have a lot in common.

The Slave

When a man is a slave, he is a submissive who gives up his power to a dominant Queen or master. A slave becomes viewed as their dominant's property. He has willingly abdicated his freedom, which is different than the traditional use of the word "slave." As a slave, a man still gives his consent to be completely controlled by the Queen. She dictates every aspect of his life with very little input from him. Slaves are responsible for meeting all their Queen's needs and wants. They attend to their sexual needs, prepare their meals, keep their houses clean, and provide emotional support and company. Queens may make their slaves entertain their friends or serve others during events or parties.

Slaves may be walked around with collars on a leash. This role is reserved for more intense versions of femdom. Some men may want to add aspects of slave and slave training to a submissive role in a Female Led Relationship, but a true slave is generally in this role and under the control of his Queen

24/7/365. Now you may ask yourself why any man would want to assume this extreme position. It's simply that he desires the experience of complete submission, where he prefers to be controlled and have every decision and aspect of his life controlled by his Queen.

In many ways, men feel extremely free. Free from the stresses in life of making decisions, setting goals, planning, and executing. A slave just does what the Queen orders him to do, and he lives to fulfill all of her desires. Slaves are often totally subservient to their dominant partners. They must ask permission before they do anything and be available for whatever the dominant requests. They must complete daily chores and work hard for their dominant's approval. Slaves are often subject to punishment if they deviate from their duties. They may also receive rewards for good work, such as completing all their chores for the day or maintaining good behavior for an extended period.

Relationships between slaves and their Queens may vary. Some relationships allow for more negotiating than others. Some slaves enter into slave contracts where everything is specifically laid out and rules are written, whereas others prefer to change things as they go along. The important thing for you and your Queen to decide is how much control she will have over you, and you must ensure that this is indeed the role you wish to play in her life. Once these decisions are made and agreements are set, life tends to go much smoother.

CHAPTER 6
Why Do Men Like Submission?

Why do men like to be submissive? From childhood, men were taught to respect their mothers, who will remain a dominant female figure in their lives. Men have also always been fascinated by the power of a strong woman for decades. I believe that a man's true nature is his deepest desire to submit to a powerful Queen. He will fight it, ignore it, or hate it because of patriarchal conditioning, but once he recognizes that female dominance is what he craves, he embraces it and is set free. He is able to express his innermost fantasies, and we see this more in social media postings and in their porn choices.

Why is Femdom porn exploding at almost one million searches a month if it were not for the increased desire for female domination? Men's true desires are expressed in their fantasies, and they explore these fantasies through porn consumption when there is an absence of a strong dominant woman in their lives. A man learns early on that complete submission to a Queen is what he desires most in life and because he is constantly searching for his life purpose. Submission aligns with his deepest desires to surrender to a powerful Queen.

From the dawn of time, men went out into the wild, faced grave danger, hunted, and provided for their families. Why? Because he knows he serves and protects his Queen through this daily routine. Men were expected to go to war and fight in armies, which he did to fulfill his duty to protect the Queen. If men did not have this inner desire to serve and protect women, women would have been trained a long time ago to do the same. A man shows his ultimate submission through service to his Queen.

Men who are submissive tend to willingly have the desire to submit to the authority of someone else, like his Queen. They're comfortable in this role and have a service-oriented mindset, finding peace in taking instructions from his Queen who he respects and admires. Healthy submissive relationships are both conscious and consensual. The submissive man makes a conscious decision that this is the life he wants to lead. In all relationships, romantic or professional, there is always one person who has agreed to have the power to lead and make decisions. We see this in corporations, countries, governments, and now the home.

There is a significant amount of trust for the submissive man to consent to abide by the rules of his Queen, and he feels no threat to his value because it is what he chooses.

For men, to be submissive is their greatest fantasies come to life. A man's desire to be dominated by a great woman is so strong he willingly begins his exploration by submitting to a dominatrix. He will explore pain, submit to your whims, and even pay to feel the fear and excitement of being dominated. The thrill of the unknown and the anticipation is all just too irresistible for him. Men's fantasies are expressions of their innermost desires, so each session with his Queen involving domination and submission triggers him and allows him to fully explore his deepest desires. When a man finally finds the Queen of his dreams, he can now move from intermittent triggers in domination and submission sessions to daily life. He now gets to live his true submission fantasies every single day.

What could be better than a relationship with the dominant Queen of his dreams and an opportunity to explore female led life each day? I believe that it is unhealthy for men to suppress these urges and never have an opportunity to experience their desire to submit to a Queen due to patriarchal conditioning or a belief that being submissive is taboo. It's important to understand the submissive male to comprehend how the female domination lifestyle is fulfilling to him.

Not every female domination relationship is the same. Some are more advanced than others based on the desires of the individuals involved. Some couples keep it confined to the bedroom, and it is here that men get to experience great sexual arousal from being sexually dominated by a strong woman. You'll enjoy being pinned down while blindfolded, and your Queen gets on top and spanks you. Whatever your Queen wishes will be done.

More couples are adding female domination to spice up their sex lives. Others take it outside the bedroom and into their everyday life. To these couples, female domination and male submission are more of a lifestyle and a belief system. Regardless of the activities, I have found that a majority of the couples who are in Female Led Relationships have better marriages and relationships. They also seem to enjoy deeper intimacy and more fulfilling sex lives.

As part of submission, some men also desire punishment, such as spanking and whipping, forced feminization, dressing in women's clothing, being treated like a weak, pathetic sissy, humiliation, pegging, water sports (e.g., forced enemas or golden showers), chastity (e.g., wearing the chastity cage), confinement (e.g., being locked in a cage), and more. The range of domination will vary from couple to couple, so it's integral to be very clear about the level of domination you desire and communicate with your Queen right from the start.

At the heart of it all is that men want to worship their woman by tending to her physical and sexual needs, and they are willing to be made into domesticated servants to their Queens. Above all, men long for a powerful, superior woman to whom they can completely surrender and devote their lives to service. Why else do many choose women who are most like their mothers for long-term relationships? They want to look up to a Queen, be led by her, and serve her in their most private moments.

Men cannot resist an intelligent woman who holds herself to the standard of Queen in all things. It isn't the money spent on a Queen that is the point, but rather that for centuries, powerful women have been able to control powerful men and bring them to their knees in acts of complete submission and surrender. We think of Cleopatra, Anne Boleyn, Queen Elizabeth I, Catherine the Great, and so many more. Men desire women who fulfill their dreams of a powerful Queen to direct, lead and love them but who accept them for who they are.

CHAPTER 7
Why Do Men Desire a Queen?

What makes a woman who is a Queen so desirable? What are some of the qualities they possess over all other women? A Queen is a high-value woman, and she is very aware of who she is. She exudes confidence and grace in everything she does. Some women in the past who would be considered Queens are Grace Kelly, the late Queen Elizabeth II, Elizabeth Taylor, and even Princess Diana. These Queens possess strength of character and people gravitate toward them. Women who are Queens adopt a similar attitude and they are generally very inspiring to both women and the men who choose to submit to them.

A high-value woman is not afraid to stand up for what she believes in, irrespective of everyone's opinions. One of the qualities that makes a Queen so desirable is her ability to be self-sufficient. Many men love ladies who can take care of themselves without any help. Additionally, she is kind, confident, inspiring, bold, truthful, dedicated, and honest. Queens are attractive to men because they don't compromise on their principles by following others blindly. She makes her opinion known and backs her claims with facts. But she is also open to being corrected when it is the right thing to do. What you love about Queens and why you crave a Female Led Relationship are as follows:

Kindness

Compassion is one of the most potent weapons that high-value Queens wield. She does not look down on anyone because she is confident in her own abilities and knows how to treat others. She is regal. Therefore, she uses her kind heart to help people rather than tear them down. Look at the greatest monarchs and Queens of all time. Why were they loved? Because they were kind and compassionate. I always thought the late princess Diana would make an exceptional Queen because she had such a kind heart and was truly loved by the people.

Interesting

Queens never stop learning or placing a high value on self-improvement and you as her submissive gentleman will feel this passion and zest for life. It will be infectious, and it is what makes you so obsessed with her. You can be married or together for 1 year or 20 years, and she will still be an obsession for you once you bond in a Female Led Relationship. You will always find a Queen in interesting places — traveling, museums, events, conventions, cooking or art classes, CrossFit, or doing extreme sports.

Queens believe in challenging themselves and they are not afraid to go out and learn new things. Men are always eager to find a Queen, but once you've found her, how to keep up with her will be your challenge. Queens require a man who can keep up and support them in their interests. If you enjoy sitting at home playing video games and drinking beer, a Queen is probably not for you. High-value women seek men who can have a purpose in their lives so it's important for you to also have similar interests.

High Self-Esteem

A Queen carries herself differently. She has high self-esteem and believes in herself. She will not allow anyone to treat her less.

Such women have usually spent time working to be the best version of themselves daily. They put time and energy into achievements and many are very successful. A Queen needs a man who will show her the respect she deserves because she has earned it. She is confident in her own life, and she will expect you to be supportive in her pursuit of success.

Great Communication Skills

You will notice that your Queen will have above average communication skills and will not be afraid to discuss things.

When expressing her emotions and thoughts vocally, she does not hesitate. If she knows that she might offend others, she will be diplomatic while expressing herself. Similarly, when it comes to requesting something that will be beneficial to her, she is always bold to speak her mind. This is what makes a Queen so interesting to be with in a relationship. She will have no issues in dominating you as she is accustomed to giving orders and discussing all issues. Communication is key in any great marriage or relationship, so it is important to be with a woman who is great with communication.

Queens Never Surrender

When it comes to pursuing their dreams, Queens don't give up. They are in it for the long term and they often know precisely what they want out of men, out of life, and out of love. This is why your Queen needs your full support to be your best. You have a real part to play in her evolution and vice versa. There is real growth in your union, which is why a FLR or female led marriage is such an enriching and transformative experience. Your sole purpose in life is to be the best submissive supportive gentleman you can be and learn to support your Queen so that she can step into her power and be the great leader she can be.

CHAPTER 8
Responsibilities of the Queen

As you have seen, the Queen has an especially important role in the Female Led Relationship where she controls and leads the household. To do this effectively, she must take care of her responsibilities. The roles and responsibilities of your Queen as the dominant in a healthy relationship are:

To Nurture

Your Queen's role is to nurture your naturally submissive instincts, helping you to learn how to serve her but not in a way that exploits you or is emotionally abusive. Your Queen must hold herself to the highest standards, especially when she expects the same from her submissive man.

She Takes Responsibility

It's important that your Queen takes responsibility for everything she orders and requests of you. She accepts your role and how she is allowed to be in it. She acknowledges your strengths but also your weaknesses. She accepts when things go wrong and apologizes when needed. She must realize that with great leadership comes great responsibility, and it's never to be taken lightly.

She Is Emotionally Resilient

The Queen must remain calm, cool, and collected. When things go wrong in life, as they always do, she doesn't lose control or blame those around her. She must remain positive and driven to work things out. She strives to overcome obstacles and succeed in all aspects of his life. She must never mistake emotional resilience for never showing emotions. But she should do so in a controlled manner, in a way that doesn't harm others physically or emotionally.

She Leads

The Queen's in charge. She leads from the front, in all areas of her life, and especially when interacting with you, the submissive. That doesn't mean she doesn't listen to your opinion or take your advice. She absolutely does and grows as a person by doing so. She leads without being a dictator. Instead, she uses her dominance to encourage, challenge, support, and lightly push when she sees your submissive nature holding you back or stopping you from achieving what she wants. The best leaders are those who compromise, negotiate, and listen.

She Commands Respect

A dominant Queen must earn the respect of her submissive. She must trust, like, and have chosen to respect you. Being a submissive means you are choosing to put yourself in a potentially vulnerable position. A dominant Queen must work to build a strong bond of mutual trust and respect as a foundation of the D/S dynamic.

She Communicates Well

Female Led Relationships do not work without good communication. Period. Being a good communicator means the Queen must be able to listen and read her submissive's nonverbal body language, be direct when needed, and speak with clarity in a warm, friendly, and empathetic manner. You must also be willing to accept feedback and adapt your behavior when necessary.

She Sets the Rules

Perhaps the most obvious role of the dominant Queen is that she sets the rules, laying out how she likes things to be done. Some domination and submission dynamics remain in the bedroom, in which case the dominant would be the one ordering the submissive to adopt positions, and what she may and may not do. If your dynamic extends beyond sex, then you might have other rules set, such as you being responsible for the household, or her fetching you a drink when thirsty, or allowing you to order for your Queen at a restaurant.

She Disciplines

Some submissive men enjoy the feeling of being disciplined when they mess up or will act bratty to force the Queen into punishing them and showing dominance. I believe that some submissive men may even do this unconsciously as behavior stemming from childhood acts when they tried to get their mother's attention. A show of power and strength is a turn-on because it's primal. You know your Queen has the confidence and assertiveness, and she can be the powerful dominant force you require.

This discipline you crave can be light "funishment" like getting tied up and spanked with a flogger. Some Queens may require a more serious form of discipline for which there needs to be consent. This may include caging, caning, use of a cross, addition of more duties, assuming positions like "man table" for hours, or servicing her and her friends. As long as there is an agreement, couples can take discipline to any level they want.

She Ensures Her Submissive Is Cared For

Just because you enjoy serving your Queen or being the one with less power in the dynamic, that does not mean your Queen can treat you badly. In fact, she needs to ensure your needs are being met as well. The exchange you make is that you willingly consent to anything she desires to do to you, but she needs to take care of what she requests of you and ensure they do not push past your limits and boundaries. If you have a BDSM session, aftercare is very important. I discuss these issues more in-depth in my book *Femdom*.

Part of your Queen's responsibilities as the leader is to ensure you are both getting what you need out of the partnership. This is why communication is so important. You need to be able to step out of the power dynamic in order to have important discussions. She should not be forcing you to do things by using aggressive behavior with no regard for your safety, unless this is what you have agreed to.

It is important to understand that as a submissive you still have the responsibility to govern your own life. You are not living to be a doormat or a pushover, waiting to be abused. There must be a give and take in any relationship, and you and your Queen must communicate on limits, boundaries, and safe words. It is also not your Queen's responsibility to dictate what you do in life regarding your career, your goals, or your likes and dislikes. All must be respected. As head of the household, she makes the decisions with your say. Your role is to fully support your Queen in a committed, dedicated manner and to always show respect. If there are any relationship or marital disagreements, you agree to communicate and discuss all issues openly and respectfully.

CHAPTER 9
Benefits of a Female Led Relationship

There are numerous benefits of a Female Led Relationship. First, a relationship where the female is leading the household ensures that the household thrives from streamlined decision-making and runs smoothly. There is a great scene in the successful show *Animal Kingdom* in which the matriarch in the family keeps everything together, and once she dies, the entire family unit collapses and everything is on the brink of destruction within a couple of months. It highlights the great power of women to keep everything under control.

In relationships, consensus and acceptance are never good approaches to decision-making as it leads to compromise. Compromise means that neither you nor your Queen is 100 percent happy, and any decision is less than optimal. Empowering the wife or girlfriend to make all the decisions brings order, stability, and predictability to a relationship. More than anything, it ensures a lack of dispute and argument, which results in a harmonious union. Research on leadership is finding that women make better leaders at work, so why not in the household? Leadership is one's ability to influence others to achieve common goals. To accomplish this, a leader needs to possess skills that can effectively communicate goals, motivate others, help others improve, give support when needed, and ensure the well-being of everyone involved.

Women are better at both communicating with others and showing consideration, and this goes a long way toward ensuring a calm and happy household. In addition, men have found that when they assume the role of serving their women, they feel empowered because their women feel much happier and supported for being able to get what they want. The Female Led Relationship is a win-win situation for both. The outcome is fewer headaches, arguments, and disagreements, giving more time to having fun and feeling connected with open communication.

I discovered that couples in a Female Led Relationship experience more harmony because each person is clear on their roles and code of conduct. Your Queen will make sure that what needs to be done in your home is done at the right time, completed in the right order, and is performed well. In any wife led marriage, she decides what is important for her man to do at any given time. If the man is in agreement, then the relationship will be smooth.

However, the challenge occurs when women and men are unsure of their roles, and this struggle exists when couples want "equality" in a relationship. I often have this conversation with my friends who are leaders and professionals in their careers. How often does anything get accomplished if everyone in the firm is equal and there is no leader? They usually never agree. It's the same with relationships. Women have been led to believe that the best we can hope for is equality, but equality leads to disagreement.

At some point, someone needs to take leadership in making the decisions and managing the day-to-day activities in the relationship. There can be understandings and "suggestions" by both partners, but, in general, leadership is necessary. The woman must have the final say. Men submit to their women as a knight would to his Queen. Generally, women are more adept at leading at home, and they make most of the decisions, even in traditional marriages. So, for men, this is often easily accepted as the way it should be. In FLR, it is enhanced because the woman knows she has a supportive, obedient partner. This obedience only makes the woman happier and more loving to her man.

In 2021, I released my book *Mommy's in Charge* to help parents with teaching their kids about female led and female empowerment. When a mom is leading, she is inspiring the younger generation and the entire household is prepared for the challenges of living in a society that will eventually be run by women. It's more than likely that your children will be managed by female bosses and will experience female leadership in the future. Research shows that 40 percent of households are run by women and 37 percent make more than their husbands.

Thirty years ago, in married, heterosexual households, a male partner was generally the primary breadwinner and considered the head of household. Even among married two-earner households, it is increasingly common to see women as the head. Among married households, the share of women heads of household increased 24.3 percentage points, from

50

21.8 percent in 1990 to 46.1 percent in 2019. To demonstrate the growth of female led, in 1990, only 32.5 percent of households were headed by women.

Over the next three decades, the share of households headed by women increased by 17 percentage points, and by 2019, households headed by women accounted for half of all households. Education has a big part to play where over the past 30 years, the share of women who are heads of household and have a bachelor's degree increased from 17 percent to 35 percent. Despite the shrinking education gap, women still earn less than men. The median income of households headed by women is almost $20,000 lower than those headed by men. There is no question that females are taking charge of households and are becoming more influential in the modern family and the workforce, which changes the dynamic of relationships and marriages.

Balancing Feminine and Masculine Energy

Men are actually attracted to women because of their divine feminine energy. This is due to the influence and power of sexual polarity. Polarity essentially means opposites. In terms of attraction, this means that the divine feminine is attracted to the divine masculine, and vice versa. What makes a Female Led Relationship or female led marriage so much more superior to a male led relationship is the Queen's leadership and dominance that can help balance feminine and masculine energies. As she embodies the sacred feminine, she will be operating from her feminine power.

The feminine is the Mother. She is the creator, giver, and bearer of life. The feminine is the carer, the maternal figure

51

who loves unconditionally and wholeheartedly. A feminine woman is dynamic, flowing, and always moving. This woman said to be in her feminine is in a state of flow. Feminine energy is no less powerful. We think of the power of Mother Nature and the impacts we have witnessed on the Earth.

Both men and women have masculine and feminine energy within them. Usually, a person tends to lean more toward one side than the other. Masculine energy traits are presence, confidence, logic, rational, security, honesty, trustworthiness, reliability, achieving, and dominant. Feminine energy traits are dynamic, flowing, receptive, open, intuitive, trusting, creative, passive, authentic, caring, vulnerable, and supportive.

A strong Queen can help to balance both sides of this energy in men. Hence, they create a more harmonious existence in your female led relationship. Feminine energy is centered around values such as love, kindness, and partnership. Contrastingly, masculine energy values organization, structure, routine, achievement, and rigidity. Both need to be cultivated daily. The power of merging the two is when there is a polarity between two people, we experience the meeting of both yin and yang energies. There is mutual cooperation and balance. Deep sexual intimacy is abundant. Sexual chemistry flows. Lovemaking is intensely passionate, steamy, and wild.

Harmony exists when feminine energy is balanced with masculine energy. There is flow, smoothness, and intense attraction, which is why these unions are so successful and long-lasting.

CHAPTER 10
Rules in a Female Led Relationship

Establishing rules and guidelines from the beginning will help make the relationship successful and give both partners a clear outline of how things will be, so everyone knows what to expect. The Queen lays out the rules and can choose to post the list for your daily reference. Once the Queen sets the rules, you will be required to follow them, so it is imperative that you agree to them and have detailed discussions about them. Your Queen is now your sole authority figure. You will show your devotion to her command by following the rules. This is what makes Female Led Relationships different from male led relationships because everyone knows their role and the rules help things run smoothly.

The rules of a Female Led Relationship are established to ensure you have guidelines on how to thrive in your relationship. Here are some guidelines that need to be followed:

1. Understanding roles and boundaries

Both you and your Queen need to be comfortable and happy with the setup of a relationship. The best way is to ensure the roles in the relationship are clear, and both partners accept their roles and know where the boundaries are drawn. Communication about who will take care of responsibilities and clearly outlining duties and roles for both of you is crucial. You want to ensure that you are both on the same page before you dive into female led life. Once roles and boundaries are established, there are fewer arguments.

2. Transparency and honesty

For any relationship, transparency and honesty are both incredibly important. You and your partner should feel comfortable approaching each other if there are issues with the setup of the relationship. Both you and your Queen need to feel heard and free to express your feelings and concerns. I always suggest that couples have a discussion hour once a week when an open discussion is encouraged. Sunday evening or morning over brunch is ideal, so you start the week off right. You and your Queen take turns discussing the relationship, your experiences, desires, issues, and hesitations. Refrain from being critical and never interrupt your Queen when she is speaking.

3. Review the relationship

It is rare that two people know exactly what they want. A Female Led Relationship might be working now, but it might not be what works forever. Take the time to review your relationship periodically, making sure everyone is happy. If you are following the weekly discussion period, this can be very helpful. Otherwise, once every few weeks is mandatory to discuss your relationship.

4. Remember the love

A Female Led Relationship isn't about power, but it is a structure to follow for two people who love each other. Don't fall into the trap of being more concerned with your role than what you feel for your partner. Make decisions because you love each other. Focus on the love and the connection you have built. Sometimes we take for granted our relationships or marriages, and we fail to see the bigger picture. It is important to remember the love and the real reasons you are together.

5. Ignore opinions

One thing that stays constant is everyone has an opinion. But what's right for one couple may not work for others. Ignore the critics. You and your Queen know what's best for your lives. Don't allow the opinions and criticisms of others to hinder your exploration and what you and your Queen decide to pursue. Self-acceptance has become a popular theme today, and this applies to relationships as well. Accept your limitations and be honest about strengths and weaknesses and communicate about them. No other person can comment on what works for you and your Queen, so be true to your own goals and desires.

The Queen's Rules for Her Supportive Gentleman

1. The Queen makes the rules.

2. Your Queen creates a list of rules, chores, and regulations for you to follow. They should be reviewed regularly together. This helps to set the expectations and parameters of the relationship.

3. Establish yourself as a masculine "Knight" figure. She will be your Queen and you are her knight, which means your purpose in life is to support her and be at her side. You should address her as "Queen," "Mistress," and "Goddess" as much as possible.

4. Be respectful of her wishes and desires at all times, even when you disagree. Allow her to express her views and listen intently. This is not always easy for men, as you will want to go into a defensive, guarded, and silent position when confronted. Generally, women want to be heard, and they often need a good listener. So, be that confidant for her—someone who she can discuss any issue openly.

5. Keep up with your chores without the need for constant reminders. If she decides that your duties include taking out the garbage and doing the dishes, do them each day without having to be reminded. Your goal is to reduce her responsibility with the domestic chores. Feel free to add some chores and surprise her from time to time.

6. Be attractive to your Queen. Try to present yourself the way she prefers. If she likes a beard or goatee, then try to grow one. If she prefers a lean muscular body, then

try to lose weight and tone up. The idea is that you must be attractive to each other to keep the attraction alive. This is more important for you, her submissive, as you follow the rules she makes. Just because she is in charge does not release her from the same responsibility to keep the sexiness alive.

7. In a Female Led Relationship, the number one rule is sex is for the Queen's pleasure, so you will need to ensure you are well prepared with tips and techniques on how to turn her on. Do you know how to pleasure her properly? If your skills are not up to her standards, then get my book *Oral Sex for Women* and brush up on your skills. Are you a great lover? Do you switch things up, change up your technique for intercourse, oral sex, and foreplay? Knowing how to pleasure your Queen is mandatory.

8. Engage in discussions about your fantasies and what really turns her on. If you've been with your Queen for years, there might be all sorts of sexual fantasies that she has waiting for you both to explore. Since everything requires mutual consent, it will be important for both of you to be completely honest about your wants and desires.

9. Your Queen makes the decisions about sex. She decides when, where, and how you have sex. She may decide to put you in chastity or demand that you come only when she commands. You are free to add some ideas, but generally, you will obey her. If she wants oral sex, you perform it. If she wants kissing and foreplay all night, the answer is the same: "Yes, my Queen." You ask her when you want to orgasm: "May

I orgasm tonight?" You never ever ejaculate on her face, body, or anywhere else unless she gives her consent. If she wants to give you fellatio, she decides how long and if she does it at all. It should never be assumed. You will ask her how she wants to be pleasured each day. These are things you will need to discuss with her in an open conversation. If your Queen forbids you from masturbating, you must stop. This is the difference with a Female Led Relationship — you must take your orders from her. Any argument and objections mean you are not really practicing FLR. Now, does this mean there is no mutual consent? Absolutely not. You must voice any and all concerns. You both need to encourage open and honest communication.

10. Compliment your Queen. Flattery will get you everywhere. You and your Queen are the only ones who can pump each other up, and for your Queen to be inspired to take on the leadership role, she will need plenty of encouragement from you. Men often reveal that they never feel compelled to compliment their partners because the woman should already know that the man loves her, but human beings need to be reassured, and your Queen needs to hear that you appreciate and love her each and every day.

11. Most men think women don't want sex as much until they meet one who does. Your biggest problem will come from keeping up with her unleashed desires. The truth is that many women don't want sex often because selfish, untrained men are not satisfying them. When you focus on her pleasure — and she is thoroughly

enjoying and participating in sex — you'll see her desire to constantly be intimate.When you start focusing 100 percent on her pleasure, and she knows that sex is for her enjoyment, she will want it much more often.

12. Becoming the right partner and getting plenty of practice will help you learn to become comfortable enough in your skin to fully appreciate the wonder that is the oral orgasm. Learning to make her feel good will make you a better man and more confident, which ultimately will make you more likely to feel satisfied. Needless to say, the more often you experience orally pleasuring your Queen, the more quickly you'll achieve the female led attitude that your pleasure comes from giving pleasure. Your pleasure will come from orgasming her as much as possible, and you will have an unbelievable sense of satisfaction. The goal of your intimacy should be to satisfy both of you, placing the focus on her first.

13. Your Queen will probably want to take control over the finances and your earnings. Female led women are usually strong capable women, and they often want to control the finances. Your Queen may decide to leave you in control of the money, otherwise, she may give you an allowance and take control of it all. This does not mean you won't make decisions together about major purchases of how to handle taxes, etc. On the contrary — both of you can feel like you have a voice in what happens. All too often in traditional relationships, men control the finances, and they may or may not be adept and successful in financial management. When women control the finances, she

feels a greater sense of authority and power, and you naturally become more submissive and obedient.

14. When it comes to social activities, your Queen makes the final decision and sets the schedule of activities for the family. She decides where you will go, on what days, and what events and activities are appropriate for the kids. But you must also offer your input in a respectful manner. For example, if going to the movies, the Queen decides what to watch, where to sit, and the type of snacks to eat and drink. If she decides to allow you to make decisions, it is still up to you to ask what she wants and to get it. The idea is that you surrender to her decisions, but you support her by taking care of things and offering your help. All too often, I witness women dragging shopping bags or having to get all of the family snacks, stumbling over people in a theater with no help from her partner. It is the opposite in a Female Led Relationship, and you are supporting her every step of the way.

15. Obedience 24/7/365 is the foundation of any FLR. Discipline is, therefore, a necessary element of the relationship to ensure you comply with your Queen's wishes. Verbal discipline is the way I choose to ensure obedience, but physical discipline is also part of the teaching if it suits the *Love & Obey* Queen. Disobedience will be met with strict discipline and punishment. Your Queen may prefer physical punishment, such as spanking or slapping. This can be sexy spanking and even more regular spankings to ensure discipline on a daily basis. My book *Spanking* provides an in-depth guide to adding spanking to your

sex life or as part of daily discipline. No matter the choice, you and your Queen must discuss all boundaries and limits. Yes, you must obey her, but everything must be done with consent.

16. If your Queen requires amusement, you do it. I might order my man to crawl on the floor, kiss my feet, and then "hee-haw" like a jackass. I find it a very amusing punishment, and it gets the point across to him in a harmless and painless way that he was acting like an ass. Some men object to this, yet this was exactly a very memorable scene in the movie *9 1/2 Weeks*. She had to crawl for her man, and there were no objections raised by men or women at this time. So, this is the type of double standard that no longer exists in a Female Led Relationship.

Female Led Relationship Worksheet

There will be times when it may be wise to take stock of the relationship by communicating about the following topics. For each area, you can indicate whether it's a weakness, strength, or needs work. Sitting down together with your Queen at least once a month and reviewing these categories makes a tremendous difference to your day-to-day interaction and strengthens your bond.

Here are the categories to discuss:

Open Communication. Can you discuss things openly and freely without criticism?

Resolving Conflicts. Are you able to resolve disagreements or conflicts in a calm manner?

Activities and Events. Are you doing things together regularly?

Sex and Intimacy. Are you having sex regularly, and are you both satisfied?

Social Network. Do you both get along with each other's friends, and/or are you making new friends, particularly those who accept FLR?

Parenting. Are you happy with each other's parenting styles and roles?

Spiritual. Are you in agreement about spiritual beliefs, and do you connect over spiritual or religious beliefs?

Taking Direction from the Queen. Are you both happy with how much control the Queen has and are you helping her daily to step into her power?

Submitting to the Queen. Are you happy to submit or having issues with completely surrendering to the Queen?

You must be truthful when analyzing these areas of your relationship. Both you and your Queen need to be in sync and in agreement with anything you decide to do together. By having open and honest discussions about issues in your Female Led Relationship or female led marriage, you can identify and avoid potential disasters. Set aside time each month or more to discuss all issues and take time to really listen and connect with each other during these sessions.

CHAPTER 11
Reignite the Passion with a Female Led Relationship

Your marriage or relationship is one of the most important aspects in life. It's one where you share everything with your Queen. When you get together, you have a strong desire to be with that person. You often think about her night and day and want to spend every waking moment with her. The passion is both mental and physical; they encompass your every thought and you yearn to be with her. Unfortunately, that unbridled, untouched deep feeling can sometimes start to fade. Why does it happen and how can we reignite the passion?

Real life gets in the way, and other priorities take precedence. When you are dating, she is the focus, but as time goes on and children, friends, family, hobbies, and work are added into the mix, these parts of your lives can start to take your attention away from the Queen. Soon you are ignoring her desires and wishes in favor of your own, and soon, this escalates into forming distance between the two of you. Millions of women feel frustrated with their entire sexual lives. The extent of which emerges in some of these trends include:

- Women are more likely than men to be unsatisfied with their sex lives.

- Straight women have less orgasms than their male partners.

- And at least 40 percent of women have difficulty reaching orgasm at all.

Your mission as the supportive gentleman in a Female Led Relationship is to ensure your Queen is sexually satisfied. In the beginning, things are fresh and new. You want to look your best and try to impress her. But as time goes on, you don't feel the same pressure or desire to try your hardest. We slip into disrespectful behavior, and we behave badly. It turns into habits that eventually become common. Everything becomes routine and comfortable. The excitement fades. Boredom and monotony are the kiss of death in a relationship, and it takes real work to try to change up our routines. We adhere to the same schedules, eat the meals, watch the same show, and have sex in the same positions. Pretty soon, this boredom has you thinking of ways to change it up with outside interests or people.

The reason cheating doesn't solve anything for long is that while you change the person up, you do not change, and after a while, you get settled into a routine with your outside activities as much as your main relationship. Soon the cheating gets boring too, or worse, you get caught, and it destroys your entire marriage and life.

You get comfortable in your appearance and soon you are unattractive to your Queen, and maybe you are less interested in her. Being unattractive to your partner is the beginning of the downward spiral because once the sexual attraction is gone, interest wanes, and you are essentially friends or roommates.

Stress and Responsibilities

Let's face it, life is filled with complications, challenges, and stress. It may be bad enough that you barely have the energy to go to work and handle all the responsibilities of life, but now having to change up your marriage or relationship is another hurdle. Intimacy and connection fade as you spend less time together. Because life takes you in so many directions and a busy schedule can leave less time to do things together with your Queen, you begin to spend less and less time together, and this is where the distancing begins.

But all of this can be turned around, one step at a time as noted below.

Step 1: Get in touch with how you felt when you first met. Things were spontaneous, fun, and exciting. You were exploring each other. This is what you have to do with your Queen. Decide to force yourselves to try something new. Some couples go out and hire a sex therapist who will counsel them on certain things they can do to improve the intensity during sex. But long before this, you can make mini changes that can make all the difference.

Step 2: Focus on yourself. Have you let yourself go? When was the last time you were in the gym? If it's been a while, it may be time to revisit. When was the last time you went shopping for new gear? Or got a new hip haircut? Shave your beard or grow a beard? Maybe you liked rock climbing, surfing, or hiking — if that's the case, these are activities you need to get back to. Maybe do it with your Queen. Join a bowling league or a new church. Make some new friends. The idea is to inject newness in some form into both of your lives. Once this begins to feel inspiring, it leads to other changes. Set aside one day of the week for date night — you both go out, have a cocktail, flirt, and have some conversation with others.

Step 3: Take a trip together. Many couples take a short getaway to a sexy resort or a weekend in the Hamptons. The more you can get out of your rut of day-to-day life, the more you will begin to feel the way you did when you were dating. As a man, you only need to start doing romantic things. Make her feel special. If there's a sure shot way to get your Queen's love and attention, it is to make them feel special. Bake a cake for her, buy her favorite drink, or give a massage. Bring her flowers. Yes, she may grumble that you spent the money, but secretly she's impressed.

I can recall being at a low point in my relationship, and my partner surprised me with one night away, where he had strewn my favorite chocolate bars across the room, and the centerpiece was my favorite dessert. We spent the whole night watching all of my favorite movies and having bubble baths. It was short, but it made all the difference. It reaffirmed to me that he cared and wanted to try. If you don't try you don't succeed. Turning around a relationship can be one of the most challenging things, but it can be done.

Most couples begin a Female Led Relationship as the turnaround because the minute men begin to commit to worship their Queen, it changes everything. Have conversations laying out what your new life can look like. You have been together for a reason. Many men think that the answer lies in finding someone new, but this is not necessarily the solution, as you have not changed integral parts of your personality, so you are likely to attract exactly what you think you need to get rid of. Real change begins inside. Once you begin to change and your Queen is on board to make changes as well, the relationship undergoes transformation. A lot of what most people want can be found with your partner or spouse that you are comfortable with. You just need to take initiative to make the changes.

Another great way to change things is to start touching her again. Physical touch, whether it's kissing, handholding, hugging, or cuddling, will steam up your relationship. So, include touch in your everyday routine. Smack her butt, kiss her for no reason, touch her hand, hold hands. Explore her body and touch areas you never had before. Your familiarity after being together for some time helps you to feel comfortable trying new positions, techniques, or locations.

Sex is an essential ingredient to spice up your relationship. Don't let any excuses come in your way when it comes to having sex. If your Queen is too tired, arouse them through a sensuous massage with essential oils or light up the bedroom with aromatic candles. When was the last time you ate whip cream off of her? Combine dessert with sexy sexual exploration.

There are four types of chemistry that will help you and your Queen get the spark back in your life:

Physical chemistry: generates physical desire and arousal

Emotional chemistry: creates care, affection, and trust

Mental chemistry: generates interest, compatibility, and receptivity

Spiritual chemistry: brings respect, appreciation, and happiness

When people complain about being bored in their relationship, they often cite being stuck in a rut or routine. Then there is the worry about how to keep the relationship alive. They may feel a sudden desire for novelty and assume that novelty can only come from a new partner or moving homes. One of the biggest issues is the tendency for the primary relationship to begin to break down. Here is a summary of everything you can do to keep the spice alive in your Female Led Relationship:

Reinforce Your Relationship Daily

Remind her of the love you both feel daily. Kiss, hug, greet her as the Queen, and don't allow the relationship to take a backseat. In our busy world, we tend to place other matters above the relationship, and only when going out do we make a big deal. We make excuses for being busy, tired, or just not in the mood. Now more than ever, you both will need to spend time on the relationship.

Take Care of Your Health and Fitness

Often so much is going on that we barely have time to worry about the upkeep of our health and fitness. Only when you are healthy and feel good about yourself, can you take care of your partner. So, remember to eat right, stay fit, and sleep well. A healthy body results in a healthy mind and that clearly reflects in your relationship. Remain attractive to both of you. This increases the sexiness of all the other activities.

Spend Time Together

It is important to spend quality time together with just the two of you. Going out with the kids is not considered quality time together. You still need a date night and maybe picnics in the park, bike rides, or just hanging out. I can recall a couple who was married for 27 years and introduced all sorts of extras into the relationship, and they had lunch together every single day to simply talk. It worked. Their relationship was able to withstand any obstacle.

Give Your Queen Her Space

Being in a relationship doesn't mean that you have to be together every second of the day. She still needs to meet with her friends, and you still need the beer night with the boys. Allow each other to have time to spend alone as well.

Help with Chores

There is a reason why 80 percent of women complain about being too tired to have sex or do anything. Women have to excel in their careers and take care of the kids, the household, and your needs. It's an exhausting life. Any help you give to your Queen will help her and keep her in a sexier mood.

Make Her Feel Special

Every day is an opportunity to make your Queen feel special. You have so many chances to compliment her, leave her love notes, bring her flowers, and make her feel like she is the luckiest person in the world. Not only will she be in a better mood, but she will also respond in a positive way, and it keeps the focus on you and not the cuckolding as much. The truth is, every interaction we have with another person, even someone we've known for a long time, is a new possibility for lively connection. It often takes only a small action—a sweet smile, a flirtatious look, or an act of affection to turn a mundane interaction into an exciting one. These are simple ways to make your Queen feel special. Check her out and give her that sexy look like she is the most gorgeous woman on the planet.

Keep Touching

Touch is so important in relationships. Whether it's kissing, handholding, hugging, or cuddling—all keep the spice alive. Touch her hair, her back, and her legs often. Squeeze her butt as you go by. Kiss for no reason and hold hands. Touch keeps the focus on you both.

Set the Scene

Just as you would prepare for your big night out, you also need to keep the primary space sexy. Draw her a bath, lay out some lingerie, get her favorite bubbles, get some wine or champagne, and massage oils. You want to show dedication and effort. Men always complain that they don't understand why women are upset. Women desire the fantasy of an open relationship without having to explain every step. You want to show this woman that even though you engage in open relationships, the primary relationship with her is what you need. Make a special dinner by candlelight for her. There is no need to wait for a special moment to make her feel special and loved.

Have Sex Regularly

Your sex life still needs to be great and regular. One of the first major indicators that a relationship is breaking down is the frequency of sex. So, it is very important that you have a great sex life and you keep it alive. It is recommended that your own sex be where you connect deeply as a couple. Add some oral sex or long foreplay to really connect with your Queen. Remember, getting her into the mood begins early on in the day, and you'll want to put her in the mood from the moment she wakes up. Sex is for the Queen's pleasure and focusing on bringing her as much sexual satisfaction as she requires is your mission. Even if you don't have sex, it's important to connect and work on keeping the intimacy and passion alive.

Be Truthful

Studies have found that people who are truthful about themselves experience more relationship intimacy and well-being. They also have better romantic relationships. Overall, studies find that positive connection and intimacy grow when you are transparent about what's inside of you. A recent study by the University of Georgia examined the connection between communication and the degree of satisfaction reported by couples. It found that good communication in itself could not account for how satisfied partners were with a relationship over time.

The researchers recognize that other factors must influence couples' satisfaction and that good communication can result from those factors. According to Justin Lavner, lead author of the study, more satisfied couples communicate better on average than those who are less satisfied. So, what will make you and your Queen more satisfied is the happiness you feel together and being truthful and honest about your feelings throughout your exploration.

CHAPTER 12
Compersion and the Female Led Relationship

I nterest in comparison is off the charts. Numerous researchers are now turning their focus to compersion because of its tremendous transformative effects on relationships and marriages. What is compersion? Compersion is being happy for the happiness of others. It comes into play in Female Led Relationships, because as a submissive man, your ultimate goal is to ensure your Queen experiences all the happiness she deserves. Your duty is to ensure she's sexually fulfilled, and as the saying goes, "Happy wife, happy life." Compersion encourages authentic emotional expression, which in turn reinforces a sense of togetherness. It is the feeling of taking joy in your Queen's happiness, which is the opposite of jealousy and possessiveness.

People who experience compersion can be thought of as pioneers of significant human potential. They view others as intrinsically autonomous and self-determined — and celebrating their own unique path to fulfillment. Compersion originated with the Kerista Community in the 90s in San

Francisco, which was one of the first groups of people to openly practice polyamory. But the real foundation of compersion is from Buddhism where sympathetic joy is one of the "four immeasurable states" or qualities of the enlightened person. Along with the other three states: loving-kindness, compassion, and equanimity. According to this tradition, *muditā* remedies the illusory separateness between self and others and can therefore be a powerful vehicle on the path to liberation.

As a submissive and supportive gentleman in your Female Led Relationship, your role is to support your Queen so she can step into power and be the greatest leader she can be. You are there to be her main supporter and you are an extremely important part of her journey and sexual exploration. You are genuinely happy for her happiness. This is what makes Female Led Relationships so different from traditional male led relationships. When your goal is to ensure her complete happiness and fulfillment, it changes the dynamic of your daily interaction. You both spend your time focused on each other instead of constantly looking for what is missing in the relationship or marriage, which leads to unhappiness, jealousy, and infidelity.

Instead of each day being boring and feeling like Groundhog Day, it's an opportunity and a gift for you and your Queen to explore how to bring each other the most happiness and sexual satisfaction possible. Compersion dramatically transforms your whole life into an exciting, sexy adventure. It is a part of an alternative conception of love that is built on abundance and collaboration, rather than possession and territoriality.

Jealousy is a normal human emotion like any other, and there's nothing inherently wrong with feeling it, but it can be a relationship killer and many couples struggle with it. When it comes to relationships and marriages it becomes challenging to overcome feelings of insecurity or jealousy but the more you and your Queen work on having compersion the more happiness and contentment you will feel.

Your female led relationship should be free to evolve the way it should. You and your Queen should be free to explore your fantasies and desires without criticism or restriction. You and your Queen become facilitators of achieving your highest growth and evolution. Sometimes this growth may require the exploration of something like hotwifing. You may have a desire to see your Queen engaging sexually with another man or woman while you watch or participate, and she may have the desire to have this experience. You are required to fulfill her desires and in doing so, you fulfill your role as the perfect supportive gentleman.

As a partner in a Female Led Relationship, you are both involved in a dynamic that is internally focused and biased on mutual respect. Your Queen is the leader and you are her submissive, but you both can have compersion. In this regard, couples explore compersion with hotwifing and other activities in consensual non-monogamy. You know that your ultimate happiness comes from allowing your Queen to seek pleasure in any way she chooses. It is part of your duty to simply ensure she is happy and vice versa. She leads in the relationship, but she is equally focused on your submissive desires. You and your Queen are responsible for supporting each other's exploration and journey, no matter where it goes.

This is what makes your union so powerful and keeps things interesting.

CHAPTER 13
Female Led Relationship Sex

What is Female Led Relationship sex like? FLR sex can be the most exciting, exhilarating, and fun you've ever experienced. The reason FLR sex is so exciting to couples is because it helps unleash and free the Queen. Once women can explore their sexuality and take control in bed, they tend to enjoy sex more, and it offers infinite ways to explore all sorts of sex positions, toys, role-play, BDSM, and open relationships.

In a Female Led Relationship, the Queen isn't waiting for you to satisfy her. You must find ways to ensure that you focus on her pleasure. Sex becomes an opportunity for worshipping your Queen, and you never approach it as "wham, bam, thank you, ma'am." It is your responsibility as her supportive gentleman to give her the pleasure she deserves. Part of keeping your Queen completely satisfied, happy, and in a good mood every single day is satisfying her with great sex.

Boring sex creates boring relationships, which don't last long. Most women report being unsatisfied. Studies show that 25 percent to 74 percent of women have faked an orgasm, so chances are your Queen has as well. But think of how life would be if you gave your Queen a mind-blowing orgasm every day. Female led sex is all about how to fully satisfy your woman by placing her pleasure first. You will be making it your mission, if you choose to accept it, to make her orgasm the focus of your sex. You will become a pro at giving her the best oral sex she has ever had, which will keep her coming back for more.

Not only is this going to change the dynamics of your relationship, but you are going to reap the rewards of a happy wife, happy life. Oral sex is also crucial to your Queen's well-being and her health. You might be surprised by how much you enjoy it, not to mention the attention you get in return. You may have tried all the sex positions and role-play, but at the end of the day, you are giving your Goddess the gift that she (and her vibrator) can't give her: mind-blowing oral sex.

A significant part of finding and keeping a female led woman is that you must show complete service to her. Part of this service is being a great lover. Why has Casanova been remembered for centuries? Not because he was great at his job or could fix cars. If you're going to keep your woman happy, you will need to master the bedroom, which means becoming a pro at fully satisfying your woman.

Oral Sex

The first way you will pleasure your Queen properly and begin your Goddess worship is with oral sex. It has been around for centuries and is called by several names: cunnilingus, and slang terms like going down, going downtown, eating her out, pussy licking, sucking clam or sucking oysters, munching carpet, or perhaps some other equally ridiculous slang term commonly used to describe it. Although there are a variety of slang terms people use to describe giving oral sex pleasure to a woman, we are going to call it with the proper respect it deserves, female led oral sex.

Oral sex, to a woman, is the most important skill you will need to master if you want to call yourself a great lover. Your woman will probably orgasm more from oral sex than when having intercourse alone, and this is a win-win situation for both of you. Part of oral sex is understanding how it relates to Goddess worship and reaching the divine.

It is generally accepted that when a penis is erect or when a vagina is wet, it means a person is primed and ready for sex. This isn't always the case, yet our cultural discourse around sex and arousal has led us to incorrectly assume that a person's physical response to sexual stimulation is aligned with their level of desire.

In reality, there are many times when desire and physical arousal don't match. In fact, physical arousal is different from subjective arousal which is the active mental engagement in sex. It is this confusion that can lead to you or your Queen remaining unfulfilled and sex becoming lackluster. It is the mental engagement and deep connection along with physical intimacy that makes female led sex so exciting and desirable. If your Queen has to resort to faking orgasms or pretending to enjoy sex when she'd rather be doing anything else, this is a failure on your part and must be changed.

Oral sex done properly will change your sex life, and more importantly, your woman's sex life. Ultimately, it can make you and your woman have a great love life together, and sharing love between people is what it is all about in life. Oral sex should never be faked, played, or simulated. If you don't want to give her oral sex, it's the same as her not wanting to have intercourse with you.

You may orgasm easily during sex, but most women don't. In addition, if she's not enjoying oral sex because your technique is off or you don't know what you are doing, this can be the beginning of a disaster. Unhappy wife, disastrous life. Today, it is important for men to learn how to master oral sex if they're going to keep a strong, demanding Queen in a Female Led Relationship happy. Bad oral sex makes a woman feel uncomfortable and makes you seem unsure of yourself. Don't do as the comedian Sam Kinison instructs. He said, "You perform oral sex on a woman by writing out the letters of the alphabet with your tongue on a woman's clitoris." This gets you in the doghouse really fast and leaves you with a raging, unhappy, unsatisfied woman.

Learning how to give proper oral sex will teach you how to truly serve your Goddess and make love to her with your mouth and tongue. I will show you how to achieve a mind-blowing orgasm, which I call the *cosmic orgasm*. It is so powerful that you will feel like you're having an orgasm with her as she comes into your mouth. The Divine Oral Sex I am describing can result in true joy and spiritual orgasm that will heal your soul and make you feel like the king of the world. It will be the greatest enhancement of your love life within your present relationship and will unlock a new level of passion between you and your woman.

To become an artist and deliver divine bliss to your woman, you must be genuinely devoted to loving, obeying, and serving her and putting her pleasure first. The power of love will give you the strength, purity of heart, and connection to the feminine divine to dissolve anything and all that might still be separating you at this very moment from achieving the ultimate cosmic orgasm with your Goddess.

So, take a look inside, gentleman, observe your very own present attitude and feelings toward your present female partner, and make proper adjustments and give total freedom to your partner. Do you want to commit and make your partner fully happy right now? Do you want to make a genuine effort to achieve love, be obedient to her, and serve all her needs and bring her pleasure, or not? Do you want your partner to find true love and absolute long-lasting bliss and happiness in your relationship? If you want to unleash the real sexual beast of your Queen, then, this is how you do it.

The Female Led Relationship offers an opportunity to explore more than just a great daily life with your queen. It gives you a chance to improve all aspects of her life, making her a greater leader and a more confident woman, and connecting to her on the deepest level possible. Oral sex is the pathway to the divine. The vagina and uterus give life, and many believe it is a connection to the spiritual realm. Why is this important? Humans are not just physical creatures. We are mental, physical, and spiritual beings, and many times unhappiness in individuals and relationships can stem from the inability to satisfy all parts.

As the man in your Queen's life, you learned it was your duty to ensure your woman feels fully served. In daily life, this is accomplished by doing everything she commands and allowing her to take control of all aspects of your life. Sex is an extremely important part of your service, and now you will be able to connect to her on levels that no one else can. In the bedroom, you will now be charged with giving your Queen the ultimate sexual experience by making the sex all about her and placing the focus on her.

By doing this, you will gain great pleasure as well. You will not only feel more satisfied in your own orgasms, but you will be confident that you are solely responsible for giving her the ultimate sexual pleasure. Oral sex becomes the center of the entire sexual session because the act is the main method most women require to climax effectively. Now you have become the most important person in her life. One of the exciting parts of FLR is sharing as many new experiences in your daily life as possible.

Now, as a man, you are supporting your woman on her path to connecting to the Feminine Divine, the Divine Cosmic Force of the Universe. This divine connection will enhance your present relationship and bring new energy into your life. Tantric masters have long preached the importance of sexual energy. This is so powerful that they use it to transcend. They learn techniques to expand and deepen the orgasm experience. In female led oral sex, this is what you are doing for your Goddess.

Sex becomes the ritual you will perform throughout the entire session to help your Goddess have that mind-blowing cosmic experience together with her orgasm. Your sex becomes a ceremony, a celebration of the divine. You become more connected to the universe when you bring your Goddess to orgasm, and you are also experiencing euphoria. In tantric sex, the male energy is like fire— burning hot and fast, but a woman's energy is like water—it flows. It is this difference that makes female led oral sex so much more complex. You will no longer think of your male ego or your male pleasure. You will no longer receive oral sex or a blow job unless your Goddess desires it for her own reasons. You will now live to bring pleasure to your Goddess first. Once her needs are fulfilled, then you can fulfill yours.

The difference with focusing on her pleasure is that it takes a very precise technique to be able to get her sufficiently aroused and to ensure she is satisfied. The entire sex session is done with her at the center. I'll raise the example of Henry VIII. Only Anne Boleyn, who made Henry wait to have sex until they were married and controlled his every mood, received his undivided attention during sex. Henry had thousands of lovers who he just fucked and left, but Anne forced him to learn to seduce her and place her above even his closest advisors. This was a revolution at the time since the opinion of a woman, even at royal levels, was never considered. Women were virtually invisible. But Anne Boleyn was one of the first women at that time to essentially create a Female Led Relationship with someone who was, at the time, the most powerful man on the planet.

That is the power of female led. Once you fully commit to satisfying your Goddess, you will receive a tremendous energy boost and strengthen your worship of your Queen. I recommend performing oral sex on your woman as often as she will allow.

Traditional relationships approach oral sex as an added act, a naughty experiment in which both participants embark on a pleasure-seeking investigation. In a Female Led Relationship, it is the opposite. It is the main event, an opportunity to raise the vibration and connect to the spiritual realm. Cunnilingus can be perceived as naughty by patriarchal society, and these old-fashioned male-led couples may experiment to feel wicked about going down on a woman for a few minutes.

We see this portrayed in movies. I always find the movie *Fifty Shades of Grey* interesting. The film is promoted to be about BDSM in which the man is in control, but if you watch the finer aspects of the movie, you will see that the man is actually being controlled. Christian is giving Anna a lot of oral sex pleasure. Anna has the power in both her main relationship and the effects of driving other men crazy. There is only one scene where Christian Grey whips her, and after that, she puts a stop to it, essentially changing the relationship to be female led.

I believe that it is those finer points where Christian Grey is satisfying Anna completely, and there is much less focus on his own pleasure, though he tries to suggest that his perversion stems from the relationship with his mother. But in true FLR, the women are the power characters in that movie, which means it was much more about Female Led Relationships. So even the media recognizes that the old is out. Male-dominated, patriarchal, male led relationships are on the decline with female led on the rise, which makes it even more important for you to become a master of oral sex. Female leaders demand it, and you will need to give it.

Personally, I demand daily oral worship and praise of me as the Goddess. I see it as very crucial to my overall well-being. Oral sex changes a woman's eagerness for sex because she knows it's for her pleasure. How can you resist someone who wants to worship you? One of the greatest ways to show your devotion is to serve your woman's every desire, and this includes every sexual desire. It is important that you make her feel truly adored and worshipped during sex. You must allow her the time to relax and forget about all of the stresses of life. This is her moment of fantasy and adventure. Take her to another place with sex that fulfills her to the core.

Connecting to your Goddess's divine through the vagina helps to strengthen the relationship among many other health benefits. First, when you make sex about lovemaking and worship, orgasms are much easier to achieve and raise oxytocin, which helps to combat stress and regulate cortisol in the body. People sleep better, regulate their appetite and hormones, and report feeling happy and positive. So, when you focus on your Goddess's pleasure, you are improving all facets of her being. You are ensuring that all aspects of her life are fulfilled. Connecting to the divine through sex improves your spiritual connection and is the most powerful way to be connected.

The Female Led Relationship offers the freedom to explore with consent from both of you and with lots of communication. Even though the woman makes the rules in a Female Led Relationship, everything still requires an agreement from both of you. Women have admitted that some of the benefits are having their needs taken care of, deciding who does which chore, handling the money, and not having to ask permission for any purchase, having a greater sense of power and control than their outside life might have, and being more dominant in their sex life. Many couples in normal relationships are exploring a female led lifestyle because many men have the fantasy of serving a strong woman and being dominated by one.

In my experience, it is mostly men who first discover and want to initiate the change to female led, but once his Queen is involved, the relationship evolves quickly. Men tend to take charge during work and deal with the stress of having major responsibilities. Many are happy for their woman to take the lead at home, and they simply submit to her leadership. They look forward to when their woman comes home and tells them it's time to cook dinner, rub her feet, clean the house, or give her pleasure. It's liberating to relinquish control and give in to her every desire.

One way your Queen can be sexy while showing her dominance and leadership is by saying, "If you finish all your chores tonight, I might let you go down on me later." This is a great practice because it gives you a goal and gets you both into a sexy state of mind. Each day is a new opportunity to explore how you will serve your Queen sexually and how she can entice you to be the best lover you can be. My book *Oral Sex for Women* is the perfect in-depth guide to being an oral pro. In a Female Led Relationship, there is no "wham, bam, thank you, ma'am." Sex is for your Queen's pleasure and ensuring she is sexually satisfied is your responsibility.

Brain Vagina Connection

A woman's body was made to receive and experience pleasure. Female sexual pleasure is not just about sexuality or about pleasure. It's both, and in a Female Led Relationship, it is important to be aware of how stimulation of the vagina, breasts, and brain are all connected.

The precise locations that correspond to the vagina, cervix, and female nipples on the brain's sensory cortex have been mapped for the first time, proving that vaginal stimulation activates different brain regions to stimulate the clitoris. There is a direct link between the nipples and the genitals, which may explain why some women can orgasm through nipple stimulation alone. When women's nipples were stimulated and in addition to the chest area of the cortex lighting up, the genital area was also activated. Sex is an essential part of living a healthy life. Not only is sex great for the endocrine system but it is also necessary for your overall sense of joy, peace, creativity, and happiness. Dopamine, opioids, and oxytocin are the "pleasure cocktail" of hormones released when good sex is in motion.

When a woman has an orgasm, her brain gets a boost from the neurotransmitter dopamine. Then, in orgasm, opioids and oxytocin are also released. This experience does not just yield pleasure, it also induces specific states of mind.

In marriage, where women are encouraged to have sex, they still want to do so at lower rates. Studies show that couples who had been married for 20 years found that men wanted more sex than their wives. But is this because women's desire for sex is less or women desire good sex and the lack of sexual satisfaction makes them less interested?

Women's sexual interest is dampened by a world that sees female desire as dangerous. When women are constantly pressured to suppress their sexuality or face shaming, desire diminishes. Yet women have experienced disempowered sexuality and yet, they are still more sexually powerful. Your role as a man who must satisfy your Queen is to ensure she has adequate sexual arousal and sexual satisfaction by understanding how to give her proper pleasure from start to finish. Hence in a Female Led Relationship, sex is for the Queen's pleasure.

Domination and Submission Sex

Let's face it. Most FLR men and women have a desire to explore the domination and submission power dynamic in their personal and sex lives. Female led sex involves adding elements of D/S and BDSM and can be taken to the intensity you and your Queen desire. Female Led Relationship sex allows you to experiment with how deeply you want to explore the power exchange in the bedroom and allows the Queen to take control of you, while you learn to surrender.

Many FLR couples love adding aspects of BDSM, Femdom, spanking, and all sorts of kink play like anal play, pet play, and role-playing. You can learn a great deal about how to explore domination and submission in the bedroom in my books *Femdom* and *Spanking*. The Queen explores her deepest desires to be in complete control and you help her to step into her power by fully submitting. This allows for exciting and adventurous nights using blindfolds, restraints, bondage, whips, and sex toys. The more you encourage her bold, take-charge actions in the bedroom, the more it transfers to daily life and this is how they complement each other. A good sex life means a happy wife, and a happy wife means a happy life.

The goal of female led sex is to indulge the D/S power play and to strengthen the primary bond between you and your Queen. You can also add chastity as yet another way that your Queen can take control of you and your orgasms. Many FLR couples are eager to add cuckolding and hotwifing. Though it is not mandatory to engage in consensual nonmonogamy, many couples make the conscious choice to add in fun at swingers' parties, fetish clubs, and sex resorts to keep the spice alive. The tremendous benefit of Female Led

Relationships includes countless opportunities for you and your Queen to explore anything you ever fantasized about together, which is why it makes this union so powerful and long-lasting. It is the inward focus on each other's needs and a commitment to your responsibilities as Queen and sub, which helps form a successful partnership.

CHAPTER 14
How to Have Mind-Blowing Sex

Preparation is the key to a mind-blowing sex session. In a Female Led Relationship, sex becomes a ceremony, an opportunity to worship your Queen like a divine Goddess. Sex can become mundane and boring when you schedule around it and make it a "wham bam, thank you, ma'am" event. When sex is viewed as an opportunity for couples to fantasize, explore, push the limits, and improve love-making skills, sex becomes so much more exciting.

One of the significant moments missing in sex lives is the idea of a ceremony. Lingerie, candles, and satin sheets are all part of the ceremony. I once had a conversation with a friend on Valentine's Day Eve, and I asked her what she was preparing and wearing for her husband for Valentine's night. I asked, "What kind of lingerie will you wear?" She replied, "None." She had never owned lingerie and had been married for over twenty years. I was shocked and promptly suggested she get something super sexy for the night. In FLR, sex preparation and the ceremony of sex are very important, and it's the little things that add up to a fantastic experience.

As the Queen's servant and the man, you will need to prepare for the ceremony of oral sex. Get a nice big pillow you reserve only for sex, get a fun wedge to put her hips up on, candles, massage oils—anything you can to make the space special. Buy her sexy underwear that you'll want to feel before you begin and see her walking around in. You need to partake in making sex a special experience. Reading this book is a great start because you will be able to delight her when you can show off your oral skills.

Don't feel bad if you have all these questions in your head: "Does my woman's vagina look like a mystery down there?" "What the heck do I do?" "Where do I begin?" "What's the best area to focus on?" It can be confusing. There are inner and outer flaps and folds of skin and maybe some hair, then even more folds and more flaps, and then the flower, the bud of the clitoris. "Do I lick, kiss, give rough, soft, teasing?" You will have a million questions, and I will do my best to answer them all. But remember this one guiding principle—it all works, and you need to gauge how your Queen is turned on by it. You must become very tuned into how she is feeling.

I am amazed at how many couples never discuss sex. After a sex session, it is mandatory to ask what worked, what she liked, and did not like. During sex, it is fun to ask, "You like that?" "How does that feel?" These are the conversations to have, not just random, "Ooh, babe, I like that," or "Hit it hard." The worst is when men feel the need to talk all the way through. There is a time and place. Oral sex is when your woman wants to be relaxed, and you are modifying your technique to learn what works for her. It's not a session you are trying to get through so you can get to intercourse. You will approach oral sex like it's the main course, not the appetizer. We savor the main course in a meal like it's the best food we have ever had, and this is the approach you take when performing oral sex.

How to Set Up the Sexy Mood

One of the most important things to do with sex is to get your Goddess in the mood. Too many men underestimate the importance of this. If your Queen is stressed from her day, the first thing you want to do is get her to relax. This is the lead-up. Take over the chores — cooking dinner, doing the dishes, or other chores. Surprise her by giving her a nice bath or massaging. Let her unwind by discussing anything she wants to talk about. When she is relaxed, she is more likely to entertain having sex. I think surprises are a great way to show a woman you care, and that you are interested in fulfilling her needs.

In my past regular relationships, I cannot recall one time when my partners, even in long-term relationships, brought me flowers or some other gift for no reason. I also cannot recall a time my bath was drawn or anything was done just because. Today, this happens almost every day, without me ever having to mention it. So, when you are trying to seduce your Goddess, do the unexpected. Being excited about oral sex should delight her.

Sex therapist Megan Fleming says that "all arousal begins with relaxation." How you achieve this for your woman is important. Are you supporting her with chores and household duties? Have you placed her on a pedestal calling her your Queen or Goddess? Are you light, positive, and enthusiastic? Women are going to be much more in the mood if they don't have to come home to more stressors. It's important to begin to put your woman in the mood early in the day. Send her a text saying how much you love her and how much she turns you on. Send flowers for no reason. Meet her for a drink after work.

I have spoken with hundreds of couples in a Female Led Relationship, and many of the women admit that it is the actions of their men helping put them in the mood. Even though your woman is in charge, you are still committed to getting her relaxed, happy, and turned on to have mind-blowing sex. One ritual which must be avoided is sitting on the couch. On the night you are getting ready to worship your Queen, do anything you can to avoid sitting on the sofa watching TV. You want to draw her a bath, lay out her favorite lingerie, set the mood, and wait in the bedroom with candles, massage oil, and sex toys. She must be instructed to come to bed early so you can begin with a nice long massage and caressing. Sometimes a warm bath with candles and some wine can help get her in the mood. You will need to set this up for her. Make it a sweet surprise.

Refrain from eating a heavy dinner, so both of you can feel comfortable. Set the mood by beginning with touching her hair, kissing, and massaging. Play her favorite music, use candles with sweet scents, and do everything with care. Remove all distractions — phones, laptops, and pets, and put the kids to bed. The setup is vitally important. Date night is another way to get in the mood. Get outside the house to have some fun before returning home to serve your Queen. Keep it interesting. Change it up. No one likes the same boring routine each week, and boredom is the kiss of death for relationships.

Transform Your Bedroom for Sex

1. Make Your Bedroom Off Limits

Kids, in-laws, parents, friends, and pets should not be allowed into your bedroom, and it should remain untouchable from the outside world. Here are some ways you can ensure this:

- Place a lock on your door

- Put up blackout curtains

- Keep your phones off and out of the room

- Make sure there's no TV in the room

- Reserve your bedroom for sleep and for deeply connecting sexual intimacy

2. Add Scents

Scented candles, flowers, and scents are all great ways to enhance your bedroom and make it sexy. Try various scents on different nights to spice things up. Whether you and your man want to relax after a busy day at the office, or you both use them to wake up and energize your senses for sex and spanking, scents can make all the difference. Essential oil diffuser, some lightly scented candles, scents. And perfumes can all be great to enhance the mood. Make sure you choose them together.

3. Keep Your Bedroom at a Slightly Cooler Temperature

When it comes to the sexiness of your bedroom, the temperature definitely matters. If it's too cold, then it might limit the number of positions you can do, and the body does not warm up. If it's too hot, then it's uncomfortable for both of you. Sweating too much can kill the mood.

4. Massage Oils Are Fun

Sensual massage is one of the most efficient ways to get out of your head and into your body while simultaneously connecting with your partner and engaging in some light foreplay. Massage oils can be used in between spanking as well as before and after. It's a luxurious way to add to the sensations of the sessions.

5. Get Some Sexy Sheets

Nothing is a greater turn-on than some sexy sheets. Get a set of quality, high thread count sheets that you both will enjoy. Avoid buying white sheets because, believe it or not, stains are easily visible. Consider a sexy pattern or satin sheets so when you lie on them, they put you both in the mood.

6. Set Up a Great Music System

Music and sex both tap into very primal parts of our brain, which is why the two go so well together. It might sound like it has the potential to be cheesy, but don't knock it until you've tried it. The right music can add a whole new swagger to your mattress mambo. Choose whatever makes you feel the sexiest. Pick up a set of quality speakers and cue up your skillfully cultivated playlist, and let the sweet tunes carry you further into your body.

Tips to Spice Up Your Sex Life:

1. **Have an affair with your Queen.** Plan your date and pretend you're both having an affair with each other. Seduce each other, tease, and be sexy and adventurous.

2. **Role-play.** Dressing like another human is an easy way for all your secret desires to be achieved without an affair. Try to be a physician, patient, teacher, student, or even a soldier.

3. **Think like a kid.** As a young teenager, you may have fallen in love. But that doesn't mean now and then you shouldn't behave like one. Make yourself creative and act like you're 18 years old on the weekend. Dress like one, hang out, and become a teenager.

4. **Focus on Foreplay.** The emphasis on foreplay is one of the best ways to have great sex. Only spend fifteen more minutes getting horny before having sex. You're both going to have better sex finally. During those fifteen minutes, caress and praise one another's body.

5. **Make sex unforeseen and unforeseeable.** No matter how complicated it might seem, avoid planning sex or programming sex unless you are both busy.

6. **Be innovative and shockingly fair.** As the relationship matures, new ways to become creative must be built. Treat yourself to something that makes your heart race and your sex life super sexy.

7. **Get your bed sexy stuff**. Bring your bed with fresh anticipation. Visit your nearest pharmacy or an adult

shop and expose your senses to sex toys, lubricants, pheromones, and everything else.

8. **Feel sexy**. Look cute, and if you have to, continue to work out. Give yourself a sweet look, wear sexy lingerie, and get a new haircut. Feel sexy, and you're going to look sexy.

9. **Live the dreams of your wildest ones**. Just because you have a long-term relationship does not mean you shouldn't embrace your fantasies. Talk to your friend about it and enjoy it together.

10. **Practice withdrawal.** It'll lose its charm if you know you can have sex whenever you want. Stop having sex every now and then— and save it for days if you go clubbing or relax a bit. Plan this right, and it could be an enormous turn-on.

11. **Shock factor.** Sexually shock one another. Surprise your partner occasionally into a sexual high. Surprise him when he comes home naked or tell him that when both of you come out to dinner, you're not wearing your panties under your short skirt.

12. **Think beyond the bed.** Think beyond the bedroom. In addition to the bed, there are many enthralling areas. Think of a kitchen, couch, bathtub, patio, or swimming pool. Get creative, and it will be more fun to reward people.

13. **Add Food.** Fill the mood with food and drinks. Give meals or cook together. Aphrodisiac food will make your love more romantic and make you horny with a few drinks.

14. **Massages with sensuality**. Get naked and give one another a sex-free sensual massage. Seek pleasure and encourage your fingers to linger for a while. As long as your partner's orgasm is focused on, it will make you both feel good.

15. **Try tantric Sex.** Bring tantric sex into the bedroom for an intense and passionate sexual encounter.

16. **Think kinky.** There is nothing to remove the thrill of wild sex when the relationship starts to slow down in bed. Discuss your dreams and give life to your fetishes and extravagant wishes.

17. **Take a fun vacation from time to time.** Choose a holiday destination that you both want to visit, whether it's a crowded sex resort or a lovely idyllic paradise island. Spend all your holidays dreaming of sexy feelings.

18. **Calling and sending hot emails**. Don't wait until you seduce your partner. Just send a few sexy pictures in the middle of the day and taunt your partner if you both want to meet at night.

19. **Watch porn.** Sometimes watching porn helps both of you to get in the mood and make love better by watching a couple on the screen.

20. **Fool around**. Do not try to tie yourself up with each other for any time alone. Be loving to each other all the time and sometimes take affection to an entirely new level. If they are on the phone, take their pants off and give them an oral call in the middle of a phone call.

21. **Body play**. Instead of having sex, play with each other's bodies. Paint with glow-in-the-dark or edible colors on your partner's body.

22. **Make a video from home**. Create a video while you have sex together. Delete it or hide it in a secure place after the act has been done. Watching yourself in the video can be a massive arousal for everyone.

23. **Wear revealing clothing.** Show some bare skin, and make it look like an accident every now and then.

24. **Using mirrors.** Use full-length mirrors to increase your sexual experience alongside your bed. When you want to recreate a foursome romantic dream, you can have sex very close to the mirror. See or imagine a new pair of yourself.

25. **Make a little bit of noise.** Moaning or whispering sexy nothings in bed is an enormous turn-on that cannot be explained. Speak in bed, and in no time, you're going to wake up your partner.

26. **Sexual configuration**. Give your room a glimpse of sex. Use perfumes and candles to make lovemaking feel like a luxurious luxury.

27. **Be real.** You cannot enjoy or even be faithful to the best sex in your life until you both share thoughts and sexual memories, whether it be about a romantic obsession or a sentimental memory, with each other. Avoid being mentally awkward, and your sex relationship will flourish.

28. **Read an erotic novel together.** The spirit is our most significant sexual organ. Build and envision dreams. It's going to be a more substantial turn than you think.

29. **Creating sexual memories.** Always try something new. Having sex in a car or on a beach during a holiday, swimming nude in a pool, or even as a couple in bed. So as long as you both continuously make fresh and exciting memories, sex will never get boring.

30. **Be faithful to the relationship.** Notwithstanding love and trust in the air, nothing can tarnish your relationship more than unfaithfulness. You may go so far as to swing or engage in other kinky ideas. But as long as there is love and confidence, you can find a way to rekindle the sexual excitement without getting lost. You will probably stand the test of time if you're looking for opportunities to have better sex with your partner. Enjoy the bliss of romance and keep your passion boiling together with new and sexy things

CHAPTER 15
The Female Orgasm

As the supportive gentleman in a Female Led Relationship, it is mandatory that you understand the female orgasm. It is regarded as the peak of a woman's sexual excitement. It is a powerful feeling of physical pleasure and sensation. The female orgasm is when your Queen reaches peak pleasure. The body releases tension, and the perineal muscles, anal sphincter, and reproductive organs rhythmically contract. She will experience muscles in the vagina and anus contract approximately once a second for around five to eight times. Heart and breathing rates may increase. Before and during an orgasm, the vagina may become wet, and it may even ejaculate this fluid. Only 65 percent of heterosexual women say they always orgasm during sex, whereas 95 percent of heterosexual men say they always orgasm.

There are several types of orgasms that you may give to your Queen provided you have mastered the proper techniques. These include:

- **Clitoral orgasm:** This is when an orgasm occurs due to stimulation of the clitoris. It has been found that 60 percent of female orgasms occur due to clitoral stimulation.

- **Vaginal orgasm:** This is when an orgasm occurs vaginal stimulation or when you are penetrating your Queen. Vaginal orgasms seem to happen through indirect stimulation of the clitoris during sex.

- **Blended orgasm:** This occurs when clitoral and vaginal orgasms occur together.

- **Anal orgasm:** Some Queens can experience orgasm through ass worship.

- **G-spot orgasm:** An orgasm can occur as a result of stimulation of the G-spot.

- **Multiple orgasms:** Chances are your Queen can experience a series of orgasms over a short time.

A multiple orgasmic experience is subsequent orgasms right after the other.

How to Warm Up Your Queen for Orgasms

First things first, you need to figure out if she prefers direct or indirect stimulation, which is to say, touching the clitoris itself or through the labia and clitoral hood. You can try warming up your Queen by rubbing her clit lightly with your fingers at first, "going in a spiral type of shape around your clitoris." Then following up with oral worship. You can properly finger and stimulate her G-spot by inserting your middle finger in the vagina and feeling the front wall. You'll feel an area that's likely corrugated in texture. Stop there and use a light in and out motion to stimulate by rubbing in that area.

Blended orgasms can feel very powerful for your Queen. You can combine clitoral stimulation with some other kind of stimulation, like breast massage or G-spot stimulation. When the breasts are massaged and nipples are stimulated, oxytocin is released, which causes the same uterine and vaginal contractions associated with orgasm.

Massage her breasts, especially the area right above the areola, which many people find to be the most touch sensitive. It's best to start on the outer edges, using the backs of your fingers and circle your way slowly into the center. You can also roll the nipple between your thumb and forefinger. Some Queens love to have her man breathe on, lick, suck, or pinch the nipples. But start light as breasts are a super sensitive area. Stimulating multiple spots at the same time can make orgasm so much more enjoyable and explosive to keep her commanding you for more. Your sole duty as her supportive submissive gentleman is to be able to give your Queen the arousal and the sexual satisfaction she deserves.

CHAPTER 16
How to Perform Oral Sex

When you are ready to perform oral pleasure on your Queen, basic rules must be followed to ensure a fabulous experience. First, make sure she is in a comfortable position. Begin with light foreplay which helps her to calm down. Kiss her neck, lips, breasts, chest, and navel, making your way down. Savor each moment as though you are discovering her body for the first time. Tell her how beautiful she is, and how much you love the feel of her curves and her skin. It's going to be so much more soothing when you keep the focus on your Queen at all times. Men often underestimate the power of a compliment. Now you are going to be performing oral sex like there is a real art to it.

While you are performing oral sex, you may have a lot of thoughts going through your mind. You may wonder, "Is she enjoying it?" "Am I doing this correctly?" Be confident and look for clues. Is she relaxed? Is she moaning? Is she smiling? If she isn't, ask questions: "How is this?" "Do you like this?"

In the beginning, it should be much more like you are teasing her. You're getting her excited. You're kissing outside her panties, then slowly slipping them off. Maintain eye contact. Every movement and eye contact should be deliberate. You're watching her breathing, her noises, the look on her face. You are maintaining all the focus on her enjoyment. The idea is to slowly seduce her as you are getting her excited.

Now you are ready to give mind-blowing oral sex to your Queen. Your focus should always be on how you can connect to the divine force and energy in her, how you can get her to come alive. You want to approach her vagina as worshipping her divine center. This is how you both connect to the universal energy and it's important you always approach sex as Goddess worship. No matter what has happened during the day, she will expect a loving, sensual mood to unfold during sex and she needs to feel your confidence with giving her oral pleasure and worship.

One of the most important parts of foreplay is to place your Queen in a relaxed, happy positive mood. You want her to feel that this is the most exciting and enjoyable activity for you. Queens, regardless of experience, can be very self-conscious when a man's face is between their legs, but they quickly calm down if you approach it enthusiastically and you know what you are doing. Positive compliments will reassure her that you are eager and excited to please her. Tell her that her scent is provocative and turns you on. Once you get down there, stop for a moment and tell her that you love the way she tastes. Compliment that her pussy is fantastic, powerful, and you love everything about it. If you can convey each of these beliefs to her in a sincere way, you're going to be on your way to giving head and getting ahead.

Taking your time is another great way to help her feel more relaxed and excited about what you have in store for her.

Begin slowly. Caress, massage, kiss all around the area before diving in. Keep massaging her legs and the external areas while kissing around the vagina so she continues to warm up and relax. You need to give her time to build her divine energy, and you almost need to be going into your own state of euphoria as you perform your mind- blowing oral sex on her.

Now you are at the clitoris. This is extremely sensitive, so take care with light licks and caresses. Keep the focus on the outer areas even while you move your attention to the clitoris. The reason why oral sex is so powerful is the clitoris. It is the main region of focus of oral sex for her, but you want to take your time getting there. The clitoris is the most nerve-rich part of a woman's body. The clitoral glans contain about eight thousand nerve endings, making it the powerhouse of pleasure. To get some perspective, that's twice as many nerve endings as the penis. And its potential doesn't end there. This tiny erogenous zone spreads to fifteen thousand other nerves in the vagina area, which explains why women love oral sex so much.

We know women are all unique, and the pussy is not any different, so every woman's pussy and even their clits are distinct. Every woman needs a different kind of stimulation to feel satisfied, depending on her unique biology. For some women, it's so sensitive that they may not want it to be stimulated directly. Some women may prefer touching near and around the clitoris but not directly on it because it is simply too sensitive with direct stimulation. Other women are fine with direct stimulation and even want you to suck on it until they orgasm.

Maybe you've been confused about where her G-spot is or how to find it. This notorious pleasure zone became sensationalized back in the eighties when it was believed that if you could only access the G-spot inside the vagina, it would promote female orgasm. But now we know that some women have more sensitivity from the internal parts of the clitoral complex. That's why some women prefer vaginal penetration and intercourse more than other women. It may take a bit of time for you to learn how to stimulate all the right areas, but with practice comes perfection, which is why it is important to have regular sex and engage in oral sex with your Goddess as the focus.

Anyone can slip the penis in and move back and forth until you orgasm. It takes a real Casanova to master giving great oral sex to a Queen. My book *Oral Sex for Women* is your guide for giving your Queen the greatest oral pleasure of her life. I do a deep dive into all the tips and techniques you can add to ensure she has earth-shattering oral sex experience.

The great thing about oral pleasure is there is also the opportunity to add sex toys, which can ramp up the excitement and the intensity, plus add some variety to your lovemaking. Each night is an opportunity to try something new in female led sex.

The following are several sex toys to add to your sex sessions:

- **Vibrators** are probably the most common type of sex toy.

- **Wand vibrators** are more intense with higher RPM. They can also be great massagers for the shoulders, legs, and back.

- **Clitoral vibrators** are typically much smaller and are best for people who like direct clitoral stimulation.

- **Dildos** are meant to simulate penile penetration. They can be any length or girth. There are ones that are two inches and ones that are monster-sized. People who enjoy the feeling of being penetrated or like the feeling of fullness in their vagina or anus might enjoy dildo play.

- **Butt plugs** stimulate the ring of nerves around the anus. The difference between using a butt plug and using a dildo is where a dildo goes in and out, the butt plug just stays in and gives a sustained feeling of fullness. There are also vibrating butt plugs now available for added sensations.

- **The rabbit** toy is a combo of an external vibrator and a G-spot toy. It has an external part that usually looks like rabbit ears that provides vibration to the clitoris. And a second attachment goes inside the vagina for G-spot stimulation, so you get double the sensation. There are lots of variations in vibrators including ones that blow air, are ergonomic, and allow for dual vibration for you and your Queen to use together. In addition, try an app powered vibrator where you can control the fun.

- **Anal beads** are yet another option. Unlike butt plugs, which typically go in and stay in, anal beads provide the sensation of the anal sphincter opening and closing. Pulling them out as you orgasm can create a more intense orgasm.

- **The Waterslyde** is a long plastic slide that ties to the underside of your bathtub's spout and diverts water directly to your most intimate areas. This toy was inspired by the common practice of lying underneath the spout with your legs up in order to stimulate your genitals, which can be awkward and uncomfortable. This is something that can be used together if your bath is large enough.

- **Restraints** include wrist cuffs, ankle cuffs, and under-bed straps; this set includes all the basics. The straps are easily adjusted and the cuffs are padded, which ensures a safe and comfortable experience. If you're planning on exploring BDSM like spanking, bondage, and more, don't forget your restraints.

- **Spanking tools** consist of paddles, canes, floggers, and feathers. My book *Spanking* has all the details and is a complete guide on everything you need to create the perfect spanking and D/S BDSM experience.

Men can learn so much about how to properly pleasure a woman and there are a variety of sex tips for men, which can be followed to give your Queen the sexual satisfaction she deserves. The one thing to note about oral sex is that even though it is growing and becoming more popular, so much so that it is now depicted very often in mainstream media, women can still be hesitant about experiencing oral sex due to a variety of issues. How you handle these hesitations will dramatically affect your sex life.

Many women have convinced themselves that they don't like oral sex, and often they will try to convince their man of it too. There are also many instances of men wanting to give oral sex, but they do not know how to approach the subject or where to begin. Previously, you may have been unsure of your technique and worried about even doing it for fear of criticism from your Goddess. But all of these are just reasons based on insecurity. Once a woman feels comfortable letting you go down on her, everything changes, but the insecurities may take some time to address.

To begin with, research shows that issues over body image for both men and women are growing. When most people think of body image, they think about physical appearance and how attractive they are. But *Psychology Today* suggests that body image is our mental representation of ourselves and influences behavior, feelings, beliefs, plans, who we choose as a partner, our work, and our day-to-day interactions. So, the more that you, as the supportive gentleman, can influence your Queen's outlook and how she perceives herself, the more relaxed and happier she will be.

Women always complain about not feeling like their man truly appreciates them or finds them sexy. Women often compare themselves to other women, because deep down, they consider them to be competition. But what if you reassured your Queen daily that she is supreme and you only care about one thing: bringing her as much pleasure as possible. How would that change things for both of you? How would it transform your relationship?

Research shows that 56 percent of women are unhappy with their overall appearance — their abs and stomach, body weight, hips, and muscle. What was even more shocking was

63 percent of men also had issues with overall appearance, and similar to women, men were unhappy with their abs, chest, and muscle. Why is this important? Well, much of our behavior stems from these deep-seated issues with body image. I can recall my own experiences with being overweight and never feeling like I was good enough to be having sex with a man. I remember wearing heavy shapewear and being very paranoid when it came time for a man to discover what was under all of my clothes. I feel that it was this insecurity that may have driven me to the opposite spectrum of working out until I resembled an Olympic athlete.

Likewise, you and your Queen may be harboring some of these issues, and it is important to address and overcome them in a positive way. Serving your Queen and accepting everything about her is the first step. Critical men immediately put the woman on the defensive, and an unhappy woman means an unhappy life and sex life. A woman is much less likely to be interested in regular sex, much less experimenting with oral sex, different positions, toys, and props.

How a woman feels about her body and how she thinks you feel about her body will make a huge difference in how relaxed she is during sex to enjoy it. So, your job will entail bolstering her ego and taking note of how she feels every day. You can tell her how beautiful she is, how much you love her stomach, breasts, and thighs. You should be flirty throughout the day, not just during foreplay. Go shopping with her, help her choose sexy clothing, and be open when she expresses her insecurities. "Honey, how does my butt look in these jeans?" should be met with, "You're gorgeous," or "You look incredible." Some women may disagree with this approach, but women are suckers for flattery. That said, how you treat your Queen should never be fake or false. A smart, sophisticated woman will always know if you are lying.

Psychology Today research reveals that 89 percent of women wanted to lose weight. They also found that more than 57 percent felt inadequate in their twenties, which is when many relationships begin to form. Forty percent of women also indicated that their partner's opinion of their appearance was extremely important to body image. So, chances are, your Goddess could be unhappy with her body and will need some reassurance from you. Many women indicate that if their partner sees them as beautiful, they are more likely to feel beautiful and rely less on their own criticism. This is an opportunity for you not only to be a great lover but a great partner.

Part of being a great partner is showing unconditional support to your Goddess and accepting her for all of her strengths and weaknesses. The more you can do this in daily life, the more it spills over into your sex life. Research shows that twice as many people judge sexual experiences as a source of good feelings rather than bad. For both sexes, interpersonal and emotional factors more often serve to reinforce, not punish. This is encouraging news; it implies that there are many avenues for us to improve our feelings about our bodies.

There is no doubt that sexual experiences affect our body image, and our body image affects our sex. The less attractive you or your Queen feel, the less likely you are to enjoy the sexual experience and the less relaxed she will feel about opening up to oral sex. This affects you too since 70 percent of men say that sexual experience affects their general life and their self-image. The moral of the story is that there are several factors that can affect your relationship and your sex life, so open communication is the best way to solve many of the issues that often lead to the negativity, which eventually leads to the destruction of relationships.

Let's investigate the psychology of why women are still against oral sex and how you can help to change this. When a woman feels confident in her look, taste, and scent down there, she will even enjoy kissing her man after he goes down there. She will enjoy tasting what he just tasted and enjoy sharing the taste on his lips and her lips together after an extra wet oral sex session.

When I was working on this book, I discovered that quite a few women were very uncomfortable and got no pleasure from receiving oral sex. They are uptight about it and don't like having their men down there. They don't even understand why a man would like to go down on a woman. If they reluctantly agreed to it, they allowed it because they thought their men liked it. Even then, the women would lie passively and wait, enduring it with no pleasure until the end. I wondered how these women could not realize how great oral sex can be. I had experienced all of these incredible orgasms from it, and I couldn't imagine living without it.

Most women are lucky enough to orgasm during an initial oral sex experience. These fortunate women experience some early pleasure and learn to improve the experience each time. As a result, they increase the quality and quantity of their orgasms by naturally testing and trying different techniques and positions until they create their unique style of receiving and orgasming from oral sex. So not only do you as a man need to learn the basic techniques and positions in this book, but you need to pay attention to each woman. You have to be sensitive to each woman's style of receiving.

Some women even discover the pleasure of oral sex for the first time with another female during high school or college experimentation with girl-on-girl sex. They may test their lesbian or bisexual tendencies by taking a walk on the wild side with a lesbian friend or a bi-curious college roommate. Most lesbian and bisexual women are more than happy to help a heterosexual woman experiment. Lesbians and bi women are also enthusiastic and excited about an invitation to have sex with another woman—and that enthusiasm is a key turn-on in the oral sex.

Show her that you are eager to please her down there and offer some compliments. You must seduce her into it by being overly excited and enthusiastic about going down on her. Once you get down there and give her first oral orgasm, her opinions about oral sex will quickly change—trust me. The biggest issues with oral sex for women come from the media and advertising. Millions of dollars go into douche and tampon commercials in magazines, TV, and online. Growing up, women are taught our vaginas are nasty and dirty, stemming from decades of patriarchal conditioning and lack of research. It's horrible, but the misogynist, patriarchal-based religions and social teachings of the past few centuries have tried to convince us that the female sex organ is filthy, which we now know is medically false.

In fact, a normal healthy vagina is the cleanest place in the body. It is even cleaner than the mouth. But still, our discomfort remains, and for so many reasons. However, this social conditioning has caused millions of women to have low opinions of their pussies. They think they are smelly and gross. This same social conditioning causes many women to have a stigma against lesbians. They think lesbians are gross because they love to put their faces in pussies.

Women feel uncomfortable about the way their pussies look, smell, and taste due to being socially conditioned since they were young that it is dirty down there. It is really tragic that society would promote such a bald-faced lie simply to keep women down and destroy their self-esteem. You can actually be part of the *Love & Obey* movement, guys. You can start reconditioning your women that their pussies are beautiful. Whether your woman has more, less, or no hair, two big plump outer mounds, a set of uneven inner lips, a big or small clit — you have to love every inch of it. So, if your woman is wondering why you want to put your face between her legs and lick, kiss, and suck her down there, you need to convince her that her pussy is beautiful, smells great, and tastes delicious, and that it really turns you on to be close to her. Enthusiasm will get you everywhere.

CHAPTER 17
Sex Tips for Men

In a Female Led Relationship, rule number one is that sex is for the Queen's pleasure. How to satisfy her in bed and make sex better for her, as well as what she needs for a happy and healthy sex life, are important for you to explore. For women, everything starts and ends in the mind. Great lovers don't need techniques. They figure out what turns a woman on, and they master the simple things that give their Queens pleasure. Sex can and should be an enjoyable experience from start to finish. The uniquely intimate connection created between you and your partner begins with foreplay and lasts throughout the entire process. A great sex life can promote happiness and contentment in personal relationships and in life.

Understanding that sex is a two-way street is a great way to ensure your Queen feels fulfilled in the bedroom. Her needs and desires are equally important as your own. Sexual arousal is deeply intertwined with the body's blood flow and oxygenation. For either partner to become excited, there should be increased blood flow to the genital area. Sexual arousal is deeply intertwined with the body's blood flow and oxygenation. So, ensuring your Queen is sufficiently aroused is extremely important. My book *Oral Sex for Women* gives you an in-depth guide to tons of tips tricks and techniques you can use to give your Queen mind-blowing orgasm. Here are just a few.

First, the best way to satisfy a woman in bed is to begin by kissing her. Most women love to be kissed on the lips, boobs, neck, thighs, and just about anywhere. The more the merrier. Kissing is powerful and adds a great deal of intensity and passion to ignite her sensually. Foreplay is vital for satisfying a woman because the real pleasure points are outside her vagina.

Asking her what she wants and taking your time to give her an experience is the key to your partner's sexual fulfillment.

You need to show your passion and desire. Seduction begins in the mind and outside the bedroom; keep that in mind to make sex better for her.

When she is about to have an orgasm from oral sex, flick your tongue really fast along the length of the clitoris. Why does this work? The clitoris is much more than what you can see directly under the hood. It extends deep inside a woman's body, so when you flick your tongue quickly along its shaft, you're not only covering more territory, but you're also creating vibrations that help carry your stimulation beyond the tongue's reach.

Add in some caressing of her breasts and nipples during orgasm and as a warm-up to oral sex, and she is guaranteed to experience the most pleasure. The area surrounding erogenous zones, such as the nipples, tends to be highly sensitive. Kissing while caressing breasts are also simple ways to make her wet and to increase the stimulation during foreplay.

Another great tip is to change the rhythm of your thrusting action. Thrust shallow then deep, then thrust deep and hold. Feel her vaginal muscles contract around your penis and let her orgasm from this. Keep her guessing and wondering what new techniques you will use during each of your sessions. When a woman is pleasantly surprised by how much you enjoy bringing her pleasure, she will be much more eager to have sex.

Next, sex begins from the moment you both undress. Use this as a time to feel her body, hug her, kiss her, and massage her. You are looking deep into her eyes as you slowly take off her clothes. You are not rushing this process. Many couples who have been together for years undress and jump into bed waiting for things to begin. If you are having sex in the same positions as you do when lying in bed reading a book, this is a recipe for disaster. The Queen will expect her man to change things up. Let her get on top. Encourage different positions and change your positions during oral and penetrative sex. Sometimes she is on her back or sometimes she is in the facesitting or Queening position. Maybe she is sitting on the sofa with her legs over your shoulder. Variety is the spice of life. Adding something unpredictable can be highly erotic. Surprises are always sexy.

During oral sex, you can use your finger to provide firm pressure deep inside. The combination feels fantastic. Fingering is a great way to add some variety. After you licked her clit and she's stimulated, put a finger in her vagina and give her a few firm strokes. When she's about to climax, add a second finger.

For penetration, switch up your positions. Try doggy style, facing each other, cowgirl, reverse cowgirl, use a sex cushion to elevate her hips, lying on her back while you stand with her legs on your shoulder, up against the wall, and sex in the shower.

Next, masturbate together. Before touching each other, try touching yourselves, together. Showing each other what feels good by touching yourselves in front of each other. Watching each other masturbate gives an element of voyeurism and exhibitionism, which is so much sexier and erotic.

CHAPTER 18
Chastity and the Female Led Relationship

C hastity has become one of the biggest categories of interest in Female Led Relationships and has exploded in the last five years. Chastity is an opportunity for your Queen to be your supreme leader as now she controls when you orgasm, and you can show your true devotion to her as her submissive gentleman by following her lead. Chastity is growing because it's a relationship and sex life game changer. When you're in chastity, you feel the powerful effects of focusing only on your Queen's pleasure. Sex is for the Queen's pleasure, and this is rule number one in Female Led Relationships. But now you have the added bonus of looking forward to the reward of her allowing you out of chastity or out of the cage. It's this expression of the power dynamic that makes couples obsessed with chastity orgasm control, edging, and more.

The growth of chastity is undeniable. There are more TV shows and scenes in movies depicting it, and if you search the chastity cage on Amazon, you'll see thousands of brands and devices available for sale. One brand reported over a million devices sold in the last twelve months, which means that millions of couples are obsessed with chastity. Chastity is searched 200,000 times a month on Google. Why all the fascination? Couples have reported that chastity and orgasm control has transformed their relationship or marriage, injecting excitement, adventure, and taking intimacy to a whole new level. Who would think that millions of men would crave wearing a chastity lock for days with their Queen holding the only key?

That's real trust and devotion. Chastity means abstinence. The man refrains from sexual intercourse or having an orgasm unless the Queen gives him permission. At first glance, this may seem like the most unnatural thing in the world. Some may even think, *Why would I want to stop my man's orgasm?* This was my first thought when I was introduced to it, but after my experience and an in-depth analysis, the true power of male chastity was revealed.

Today, chastity has become a transformative experience for many relationships. At the source, and an important point for women to understand, when a man agrees to chastity, he is showing complete submission and devotion to his Queen, over and above any other undertaking in life. In addition, it gives the woman complete control over him. This is the ultimate sign of respect to the Queen and is essentially what transforms the relationship.

As part of a Female Led Relationship, male chastity becomes the major test, and many couples have reported much more intimacy and a deepening of their bond after starting chastity. Male chastity may take many forms: using a physical locking device, the chastity cage, or none at all. It may involve orgasm control, semen ejaculation control, or simply no sexual gratification at all. Some men remain locked for hours, some for days. The length of time is determined by the Queen, but like all other practices in the relationship, there must still be consent from both partners.

Chastity is not to be used as a way to punish the man. The real reason for chastity is to deepen the man's fixation on the Queen as the ultimate ruler of the relationship. She holds the key to his lock and has ultimate control. As a sexual practice in the female led lifestyle, male chastity is the crème de la crème. The Queen has ultimate control and is the supreme leader. For men in a Female Led Relationship or who crave being in one, giving the Queen this kind of control will be orgasmic in itself. It takes your arousal, sex, and daily life to a whole new level. It requires some sacrifice, but the relationship is transformed and both of you will evolve.

More couples have admitted to engaging in chastity and making it the focus in their relationships. Statistics don't lie. Male chastity is part of Female Led Relationships, and as the leader of the *Love & Obey* Female Led Movement, I can confirm that interest in a female taking the lead and the man becoming the supportive gentleman is expanding worldwide. Men contact me every day and ask questions about how to serve their Queen correctly. Today, chastity takes female led to a whole new level. In a Female Led Relationship, the desire to be controlled by a strong female becomes even more important. More women are taking control of many aspects of their lives, and many are leading countries, governments, corporations, cities, households, and now the bedroom. Part of keeping the relationship spark alive is controlling the focus of the man's desire on the Queen.

Every woman knows that men are driven by sex. It's natural for them. It is a primitive urge that's impossible for men to ignore. It is programmed in their DNA from the dawn of time. The irresistible force of their libido is like a raging fire, burning up everything that stands in the way of its desire to consume. When you are in a relationship, the Queen becomes the object of his desire. As part of a Female Led Relationship, controlling a man's orgasm is the ultimate control, and this could be why male chastity is growing exponentially.

Why do men crave chastity? I believe that it goes back to their need for attention from a strong female. Fifty percent of marriages will end in divorce, which means a significant part of the population will be raised by women. Of the households with two-parent families, many are experiencing a shift where the woman assumes control. So, children, particularly men, will crave a strong dominant female like their mothers. "Men marry their mothers" refers to the idea that more men will choose a long-term partner who exhibits similar characteristics and may even resemble their mothers. I also believe that men crave the same discipline and attention they received from a strong maternal figure. The Queen who places her man in chastity has the ultimate control, and men love this. They succumb to a strong female because it keeps the focus on them. More focus on the relationship means a stronger relationship or marriage.

In Female Led Relationships, more men have admitted that they enjoy and have a strong desire for their women to control them. For instance, placing a penis into a chastity lock where the Queen has the only key is arousing in itself. Today, more relationships are being led by women. Women are taking charge in the household and in the bedroom. Men are loving the experience of being under the spell and the dominance of women and spanking adds to the feeling of control for the Queen. When women feel empowered, they are at their best, and men get excited when they take charge and show their power. It's a win-win for most.

CHAPTER 19
Why Is Male Chastity Such a Turn-On?

Male chastity involves giving complete control to your Queen, even over your orgasms and sexual experience. She ultimately makes all of the decisions. Why is it such a turn-on? The Queen holds the key to the chastity device, and she controls orgasm. To understand what happens with male chastity, and why it's such a turn-on, it's important to look at what happens at a physiological level. Below, we will analyze the sexual response cycle.

There are four stages in the sexual response cycle:

1. **Desire:** The initial excitement phase is triggered by mental or physical stimuli with increased muscle tension, erect nipples, blood flow to genitals, vaginal lubrication, and pre-cum.

2. **Arousal:** This is the plateau phase with heightened sexual tension and sensitivity just before orgasm.

3. **Orgasm:** This is the forceful release of sexual tension resulting in muscle contractions and ejaculation; generally, only lasting a few seconds up to a minute.

4. **Resolution:** This is the state of recovery and the return to a normal state. Penises refract, but continued stimulation in some vaginas can lead to multiple orgasms.

The desire phase is the first stage, and this is where there is an increase in muscle tension, blood flow to the genitals, erect nipples, and vaginal lubrication. Things are getting heated up, and arousal begins. The arousal phase is where breathing, heart rate, and blood pressure significantly increase. The woman's clitoris becomes highly sensitive, the man's testicles retract into the scrotum, and muscle spasms may begin in the feet, face, and hands.

It is here that orgasm denial can begin. You can start by teasing and denying any touching or further arousal. Keeping you and your Queen at the height of her arousal phase for longer without getting to the orgasm phase can be enjoyable for both of you. This represents one type of chastity. Once you have satisfied your tease and denial, it's time for the orgasm phase.

This is typically the shortest of all the phases and consists of muscle contractions and ejaculation. In chastity, the Queen can deny the orgasm altogether or prolong it as long as possible. Following an orgasm, the resolution phase allows the body to slowly return to its normal state. This phase often accompanies feelings of satisfaction, intimacy, and fatigue. If no more stimulation follows an orgasm, this phase will begin immediately. The brain releases a variety of chemicals when we feel lust and attraction. Lust stimulates the production of estrogen and testosterone in the body, which increases erotic feelings and behavior.

When feeling attracted to another person, our dopamine levels surge, which is the same chemical produced when we feel good, for instance, during sexual stimulation. The more you lust and want an orgasm, the more of these chemicals circulate to keep you focused on the object of your attention, which is the Queen who holds the key to your orgasm. It is these physiological responses that make chastity so powerful because the man's whole physiological response during sex is controlled by the Queen.

Chastity is a turn-on because it immediately injects a sense of excitement and sexual tension into the relationship every day. When you and your Queen are engaged and focused on each other, with the Queen teasing and the man showing complete willpower and devotion by holding back the most powerful urge in the body, this creates a continuous feeling of heightened sexuality. Each day is exhilarating, rather than a feeling of boredom and monotony. Chastity is the furthest thing from boring, and it helps to refocus the couple's energy on themselves, which increases intimacy, communication, and connection in the relationship.

The ultimate sign of control for a Queen is to put a cage on her man. Even if it seems like fun and a distraction, it still centers the attention on him. In turn, he shows complete devotion to you as he is now yours. He submits to you controlling his every move. He can't go far and roam free with you having locked up his penis, and since you are the person who will hold the key to his freedom, you become his ultimate

Queen, Goddess, and ruler. This control of a man's manhood is a major turn-on for them.

The great philosopher Hegel said in his master-slave dialectic, "Desire plays a very important role." This philosopher stated that animals have a desire that is satisfied with an immediate object. The animal isn't aware of what it desires. However, this is different for human beings. For Hegel, history equals the history of social relations — two human desires are facing each other. What human beings really desire is to be desired by others. In other words, they want to be recognized by others. This means that human desire is fundamentally a yearning for recognition. Human beings want others to give them an autonomous value — a value that's their own and makes them different from others. This is what defines the human condition.

Therefore, according to Hegel, the main characteristic of human beings is imposing themselves on others. This is why male chastity — with the Queen imposing her will on a man and all the focus is on him while he desires her and is turned on by her controlling him — is so powerful. It goes to the heart of the social condition. The desire part, like Hegel proposes, is a fundamental need for human beings. Since the beginning of history, there have been dominators and dominated people. Due to that dominance, the master coerces the slave and forces him or her to work.

However, the master ends up depending on the slave to be able to survive. But what is important here is that even though the master is in control and holds the power, the slave is indispensable. This applies to Female Led Relationships and chastity because many opponents will argue that the Queen has all the power, but in fact, it is the man who becomes invaluable as he serves her. She needs him more now, and he fulfills his position as the supportive gentleman. Chastity takes this even further in the desire component. The basic human need is fulfilled, and the desire for the Queen and her desire to be served is what makes this so powerful for relationships. In my experience, it has the power to transform the relationship in ways that could not be achieved by counseling, retreats, or any other method.

Remember, power can be defined as the ability or capacity to direct or influence the behavior of others in a particular way. Power is not limited to domination and submission. Instead, power in relationships is understood to be the respective abilities of each person in the relationship to influence each other and direct the relationship — and this is a very complex element of romantic partnerships that are changing every day. More men want their women to have power over them. In same-sex relationships, one partner always dominates. A key component of long-term sexual satisfaction is communication. You and your partner should be comfortable discussing what you like and don't like, and personal preferences regarding how to orgasm.

Having these conversations could mean the difference between feeling frustrated and feeling satisfied. Opening the lines of communication also provides an opportunity to delve deeper into your sexuality, try new things, and fix ongoing problems. It is important to communicate at length about chastity since many men desire to have the experience and the Queen is given the feeling of complete power and control over her man.

CHAPTER 20
Types of Male Chastity

Orgasm control, which includes orgasm denial and edging, is one of the major forms of chastity. They involve the act of experiencing or allowing someone else to experience a high level of sexual arousal and pleasure for a long time without allowing an orgasm. This can be done with or without a male chastity device. For many, orgasm control is about the physical build-up and release. For others, the psychological aspect of power, control, and giving in is the hotness.

A submissive man is obedient and will do anything possible to not come until the dominant Queen gives permission or forces the orgasm. If the submissive isn't strong enough to hold the orgasm on their own, the Queen can stop the orgasm simply with a command. The fantasy of being controlled usually drives the intensity of the orgasm, coupled with anticipation and release that typically increases the strength of how the partner experiences the orgasm.

Orgasm control of your man allows you, the Queen, to experience a high level of sexual arousal and pleasure for a long time, along with multiple orgasms while not allowing the man any pleasure except the gratification he receives from pleasuring his woman. Over time, this trains the man to focus on the female's pleasure and be grateful for permission to ejaculate once in a while. It's an area of erotic experience for many in Female Led Relationships. Orgasm control also involves erotic sexual denial in which he is kept in a heightened state of sexual arousal for an extended length of time without being allowed an orgasm.

Erotic sexual denial has the power to strengthen your intimacy with your man and lead both of you to higher levels of sexual stimulation without allowing him to orgasm. In Female Led Relationships, the Queen is in charge and has all of the power to control her man. So, taking a dominant role and holding off his ejaculation for an extended time frame will give him toe-curling orgasms when you do finally take them over the edge and allow him to orgasm. Deliberately holding your man back from that explosive moment will lead to amplified erotic fantasies about you and heighten his anticipation of finally being unlocked and having sex with you—you will become his sex Goddess.

Orgasm denial can last for short or long periods, or it may be used for those who enjoy drawing out the anticipation of sexual intercourse until all other tasks or sexual acts are completed. Your man can remain locked at all times when all you desire is orgasming with oral sex stimulation. The only time to unlock your man is when you want penetration and the special satisfaction gained from sexual intercourse. All other times keep him locked, which can be minutes, days, weeks, or even months, depending on your sexual desires. If you've been dying for more oral, ladies, male chastity is one of the greatest ways to achieve this.

Every man needs to experience erotic orgasm denial. Prolonging that urge for an extended period of time can lead to dramatic amounts of sexual arousal and excitement. Prolonging a man's urge to explode goes a long way to helping the Queen to not only demonstrate her ultimate control, but he is trained to have willpower and self-control. The Queen becomes a supreme leader when she controls the driving force in a man. Even in infidelity, most men are not out just looking for pure sex.

If this were the case, most men would be seeking a prostitute. When a man cheats, he is searching for that excitement and desire missing from his current relationship. With male chastity, the Queen can control his desire just by controlling his penis and his ability to have orgasms. So male chastity can also be used as a tool to wake up a dead sex life and refocus the spotlight back on the Queen.

Types of Orgasm Control

Orgasm control can also involve additional practices like edging, peaking, or surfing. Although orgasm and ejaculation are delayed, they are eventually allowed at the end of each of these types of orgasm control. Orgasm denial prohibits men from ejaculating without the female partner's permission; however, edging is where you bring your man right to the "edge" — the brink of orgasm, only to stop or slow down stimulation before reaching the climax.

You are not completely denying the orgasm, you are prolonging the entire experience. Edging can be done through clitoral and genital stimulation, prostate massage, blowjob intercourse, or other various sexual acts — whatever gets your arousal into overload. Rile him up over and over until you finally allow him to let go. It will be intensely erotic for both partners and often leads to feeling a much more intense and high-level orgasm.

Men become better versions of themselves when they are no longer constrained by selfish, male-focused, patriarchal sex. Once he can focus his attention on pleasing you, the Queen, he has a new purpose every day in life. He can work on succeeding at serving you, and that will only work to make you happier and increase the success of your marriage or Female Led Relationship. Think of how much fun it's going to be when every sex session is controlled and both of you are exploring raising arousal and your sexual enjoyment.

Avoid Masturbation

Avoiding masturbation and watching porn are the simplest, and therefore perhaps the easiest first step in male chastity and orgasm control as well as semen retention. A well-trained man in chastity needs to learn to avoid both orgasms and ejaculation from masturbation while you administer more training during your sex sessions. This is one of the most important steps in male chastity. Uncontrolled masturbation is simply not allowed and must be restrained if men are to experience the real power of male chastity. Orgasms and even semen are for the Queen only and not to be wasted with random sessions watching porn on his computer.

Not only does masturbating while on the computer decrease his time focusing on you, but most men can become addicted, and they can eventually affect the sensitivity of his penis to arousal methods. This is similar to women addicted to their vibrators. Pretty soon, no amount of human methods can satisfy genitals that have been overstimulated with external methods. As a western society, we have allowed this to go on unchecked, but in male chastity, the foundation is to build self-control and submit to the woman's command.

Pull-Out Method

The pull-out method is considered yet another form of orgasm control, in which immediately before the man orgasms, he pulls his penis out of the vagina just before ejaculation. This was traditionally used as a method for birth control, but it is part of semen retention and thought of as orgasm control. As you will see later in the *Love & Obey* method of orgasm control, he pulls out, then performs oral sex on you until you orgasm.

Semen Retention

Semen retention is yet another form of male chastity and orgasm control. Not only can the orgasm be denied, but so too can ejaculation be avoided either through sexual abstinence or by practicing intercourse without ejaculation. Semen retention does not refer to the avoidance of male pleasure. In this practice, male pleasure is separated from ejaculation, making it possible for the man to enjoy the full pleasure of sexual intercourse without experiencing seminal ejaculation. Semen retention is an ancient practice believed to maximize male physical and spiritual energy. Much of the history appears to be rooted in Taoism.

Worldwide, this practice exists in many cultures, under different names. Practitioners attribute near-mystical superpower qualities to semen conservation, and the men who practice orgasm control rave about its benefits. They experience a notable boost in courage and self-confidence. More energy and focus and increased attractiveness to women. This makes it a contributor to male chastity, because again, the focus is on the Queen.

Some men claim to have greater mental clarity and awareness. And the motivation to do activities that are good for men like going to the gym, losing weight, increasing muscle mass, and sleeping better. They also claim to be more grounded and calmer. They say it boosts their sex drive, including harder erections, and they lose any erectile dysfunction that they had experienced.

CHAPTER 21
Why Do Women Love Chastity?

Why do women love Chastity? Women love male chastity because there is no greater sign of devotion than when a man hands over the control of his most precious power. When you place a cage on his penis, you signify that you essentially own him 100 percent. Male chastity can only work when the relationship is loving and strong, which is why a Female Led Relationship provides the perfect foundation. Your Queen has total control over your orgasm and when combined with teasing and prolonged sensation building, creates a sense of attunement between you and your Queen.

Anticipation induces an intensified experience for you with the release after prolonged build-up and it becomes an energetic release and complete feeling of power for your Queen. A woman is finally given the opportunity to be in complete control and have a man who dutifully serves her. This is a gift because we only become better versions of ourselves when we have the support we need to grow and evolve. Your man in a supportive position offers his Queen the support she needs to do what she does best—lead the relationship.

The idea that you can now take it a step further and control your man's penis is only a bonus, but it represents a very powerful step.

The first thing that happens is that every day he is in chastity ramps up the sexual focus, and it can make this process extremely exciting. When the Queen is turned on and eager to serve, this is likely to take intimacy and connectedness to a whole new level.

When a man gives up his "right" to ejaculate without his woman's permission and she allows him to have intercourse with her, both are stepping away from an old patriarchal conception of sex being performed for man's pleasure. Once your man accepts male chastity, he is accepting a new sexual role. A role in which the woman is in control and the man submits and can relax because he does not have to pretend that he is in charge anymore.

As your Female Led Relationship evolves, ejaculation itself may be separated from the couple's increasingly female-focused sexuality. A man's "need" to ejaculate is vastly overrated and a clever wife can often train her husband to come on command, once a week or month, under her supervision. The rest of the time, if she desires his oral attention and she enjoys penetration, his hard but obedient penis are all that is required for him to become your obedient sex slave. Once a man acknowledges that, he is no longer in charge of sexuality in your Female Led Relationship.

Once a man realizes that he is no longer even in charge of his ejaculations, he may be confused about his role, but trust me, he will also be relieved of performance anxiety. Male chastity will also help him retain his semen and raise his testosterone levels and sexual energy. His performance will improve, and he will more than likely be very hard and more than eager to perform for his woman when she wants to fuck him. This all helps to create the female's lead role as the man becomes the subject of her attention and enters the sub-zone where he is no longer obligated to initiate sex. In his new role, he will focus on how best to please his wife without thinking about his own pleasure because he will be aware that he's not allowed to orgasm while pleasuring his wife — except on rare occasions when she allows him his special treat.

While men may find this frustrating at first, most men are simple creatures and will soon accept their wife's complete control of their sex life. Better still, because the now dominant wife only has sex when she wants it and how she wants it. As a result, the couple will tend to be a lot more sexually satisfied. The man will quickly learn that he is now in the role of serving his woman's desires, not his own.

Men, on average, take four minutes from the point of entry until ejaculation. Women usually take around ten to eleven minutes to reach orgasm. This means there is a real need for men to slow down and for women to control their ability to orgasm in favor of their men focusing on their pleasure. Men and women travel slightly different paths to arrive at sexual desire. Esther Perel, a New York City psychotherapist, says, "I hear women say in my office that desire originates much more between the ears than between the legs." For women, there is a need for a plot — hence the romance novel. It is more about the anticipation and the longing that is the fuel for desire.

Women's desire "is more contextual, more subjective, more layered on a lattice of emotion," Perel adds. Perel also states that men, by contrast, don't need to have nearly as much imagination since sex is simpler and more straightforward for them. That doesn't mean men don't seek intimacy, love, and connection in a relationship, as women do. They just view the role of sex differently. "Women want to talk first, connect first, then have sex," Perel explains. "For men, sex is the connection. Sex is the language men use to express their tender loving vulnerable side," Perel says. "It is their language of intimacy."

Male chastity allows women to control the narrative and the lead-up to sex. By controlling their man's ability to orgasm and keeping the focus on them, they can create multiple ways to engage in romance, foreplay, and sex. It allows women to shape sex to suit their needs, which makes it more exciting for both. If the Queen is turned on, then her man is equally, if not more, motivated.

With female leadership in a relationship, the benefits don't stop at the bedroom door. A man who becomes sexually submissive to his woman will find that his sexuality and sense of masculinity will be transformed. He will become calmer and more at peace with himself. He will not have to be burdened with society's role of high sexual male expectations. He simply needs to do as he is told, and both he and his woman will be happier than they've ever imagined possible. Male chastity will make men better lovers. Once a man orgasms, the sex is usually done. By the woman not allowing or delaying the male orgasm, she essentially trains him to focus on her pleasure longer. You, the Queen, can spend more time enjoying multiple orgasms.

One of the most desirable benefits of male chastity happens shortly after the lock is shut for the first time. Once your man gets his first restricted erection after being locked, sexual tension and frustration will rise, and your sub-male will have a powerful desire to channel it somehow. Naturally, his thoughts will move toward his Key Holder. This growing sexual frustration will build, and the sub-male will find his Key Holder beyond irresistible. As the Key Holder, you will start receiving more frequent compliments, more affection, and love, and your sub-male will become more romantic. And he will have so much more gratitude when you interact with him in any way, especially sexually, even if it is only for your pleasure, like oral sex for you. Male chastity quickly creates your dream partner!

Another noticeable benefit is the higher couple's sex drive that naturally comes as a result of the greater intimacy. As the pent-up male frustration and tension continue to build, the more his behavior will be toward making you happy. Soon both of your positive feelings toward each other will begin to overflow, and the sex drive and libido will consume you both. Your man will want to pleasure you, the Key Holder, as you have propelled into the number one spot in their mind.

Instead of focusing on his own orgasm and masturbation, he is focused on everything he must do to please his Queen. This is what every woman wants. It's the dream. The longer your man is locked, the more you will shape his behavior and the better he will become at serving you. When you demand oral sex to satisfy your needs first, the more practice he will get and the better he will be. All of a sudden, the bedroom will become so much more exciting and fulfilling.

Think of it as a female sexual guarantee that helps ensure your complete sexual satisfaction. Many men experienced premature ejaculation, and male chastity and orgasm control can train them to control their release. The Men's Clinic of UCLA says delayed ejaculation is the inability of a man to achieve climax within a reasonable amount of time. Some men cannot achieve ejaculations through vaginal penetration and must rely on alternative sexual acts to climax. Some men will lose their erection before achieving the climax and be left frustrated. Some men will reach the point of orgasm but can't finish and are left feeling very uncomfortable.

Delayed ejaculation is a neurological, hormonal, and psychological event. If a man has had damage to the nerves in his pelvis or had a spinal cord injury below the lower thoracic spinal level, he may suffer from an inability to ejaculate. He lacks the nerve connection from the ejaculation nerves at the tip of his penis back to his spinal cord. More commonly, he may have a hormonal imbalance in serotonin, prolactin, or testosterone. Men taking antidepressants, whose serotonin levels are skewed by the pills, frequently suffer from delayed or loss of ejaculation. Men with low testosterone also can have difficulty ejaculating.

If men suffer from any of these conditions, chastity can divert their attention from the sex act to pleasuring their Queen or becoming aroused in other ways. Many men have reported feeling very aroused and fulfilled at the thought of just being under the Queen's control. Rather than place more stress on the man, male chastity allows him to relax and still enjoy sexual arousal and other forms of pleasure.

Lastly, masturbation can be a huge challenge for women. Many women are unhappy with the time their men spend masturbating. Men want sex more often than women at the start of a relationship, in the middle of it, and after many years of it. Men also say they want more sex partners in their lifetime and are more interested in casual sex. Men are more likely to seek sex even when it's frowned upon or even outlawed. About two-thirds say they masturbate, even though about half also say they feel guilty about it. By contrast, about 40 percent of women say they masturbate, and the frequency of masturbation is smaller among women.

The main purpose of sexuality is a union between two people who generally have some love and attraction for each other. The purpose of sexuality is abandoned in masturbation because the center of the sexual act becomes "me" instead of "we," and the person is trained to look to himself for sexual fulfillment. The gift of sexuality is misused for the sake of lifeless pleasure. When people misuse their sexuality in this way, they may begin to use pleasure to change their mood, release tension, or forget their loneliness.

Masturbation becomes an escape. It may pacify them, but it will never satisfy them. They use the fantasies of their mind and the pleasures of their body to flee from reality and the call to love. Their goal in sexual activity has been reduced to merely receiving pleasure instead of showing love. Women like chastity as a method to control their men masturbating. Chastity allows the Queen to control her man and the time he spends masturbating. In male chastity, a man's sexual energy should be reserved and focused on his woman.

CHAPTER 22
Why Do Men Love Chastity?

Why do men love male chastity? Why would he welcome having his penis locked up and engaged in male chastity? The answer may not be apparent at first. Most people new to Female Led Relationships or domination and submission may fail to understand the inner workings of chastity and find this practice to be abusive, barbaric, and downright inhumane. But just as all other practices that involve self-control and refraining from indulging in things, male chastity can lead to some very impressive and transformative results. As you have seen, at the physiological level, there are so many changes that occur.

If you ever had to go on a diet or give up drinking alcohol, the first few weeks were hell, but what happened long term? In terms of food, you lost weight and felt better, and in terms of alcohol, you felt clearer and healthier. Male chastity is similar. In many cultures, we have seen that the constant indulgence in masturbation and ejaculation leads to the depletion of life force. It's similar to fasting. Many cultures believe in a period of refraining from indulgence as a means of strengthening the body.

We have also seen how male chastity conducted in a loving relationship is transformative to men who later admit to becoming obsessed. Physically, a man feels better because his body is stronger and more energetic, and he builds willpower and even more desire for his woman. He can focus all of his attention on his Queen, which is really what he wanted all along.

What happens to men and women in male chastity is similar to what happens during dating. The man is fixated on the woman and desires sex with her, but the longer the fixation, the greater the desire. When you were dating, think of how many times you checked your phone, felt the excitement of seeing your man, and experienced little moments like the first kiss, holding hands, and the anticipation of sex. He was also 100 percent focused on you and your needs. These are just some examples that make dating so thrilling.

Once you are in a marriage or relationship for years, there is no pursuit and less desire, and eventually, both of you treat each other like an old shoe. You love your old shoe, and you would even be upset if you couldn't find your old shoe or it somehow disappeared, but it lost its novelty appeal. The anticipation, waiting, and desire for sex and togetherness are what exactly happens in male chastity when the Queen dictates when he should orgasm. Male chastity makes things new again because the woman now controls the power center of a man.

One of the fundamental aspects of social interaction is that some individuals have more influence than others. Social Power can be defined as the ability of a person to create conformity even when the people being influenced may attempt to resist those changes. Bosses have power over their workers, parents have power over their children, and, more generally, we can say that those in authority have power over their subordinates. In short, power refers to the process of social influence itself — those who have power are those most able to influence others.

The same is true when a woman has power over her man in a relationship or marriage. Men want a strong female figure in their lives, so the idea of giving up control and allowing their power centers to be controlled by a woman is very arousing. Once the Queen steps into her role as ultimate ruler and leader, the man will naturally take his position as the supporter. Ever need a man to make a grocery list on his own, then go get the groceries? He hates it. He is not interested in a leadership position in the household. Determine what he should get, give him a list, and he will gladly go do it. This is the supportive role that men would prefer to be in.

Male chastity takes the role of supportive submissive to a whole new level. All of a sudden, men view their Queens in a much different light, which is why they get instantly aroused when she places all of her attention on him and locks up his cock and holds the key. It's a symbol of ultimate control. Men also feel more testosterone, become stronger, more invigorated, and excited. His focus will naturally be on his Queen, and wearing the cage reminds him to whom he owes his allegiance.

In previous books, I have discussed the idea that men always need and respond to a leader. Without proper leadership, they feel chaotic with no direction and purpose. In the study "Sex-Role Obedience to Authority" by Geffner and Gross, obedience by male and female subjects to male and female experimenters was investigated. The four main factorial independent variables were the sex of the experimenter, the sex of the subject, and two conditions of presence or absence of a uniform presence or absence of an explanation. The results revealed there was more obedience with a uniform and more disobedience by females, which suggests that men are more likely to obey an authority figure.

Men need a purpose and a goal, so male chastity helps them to focus that purpose where it should be in all relationships — on the Queen. Think about it — are you happier in a good, fulfilling deep relationship or a bad relationship with arguments and daily power struggles? With male chastity, there is no argument, and men can do what they do best — be the supportive gentlemen. This goes to the foundation of the female led lifestyle, which is why Female Led Relationships are so successful. Men love male chastity because each day is new and unpredictable, and their Queen is focused on sex every day. When you are controlling his penis, you are in ultimate control over everyone else in his life. When he wears a cock cage, he will be thinking of you all day long.

Going back to the research on men and authority — men respond much better when there is a firm authority figure in their lives. When they are younger, this person is their mother, and maybe their father. For at least 50 percent of the men out there, with a divorce at 50 percent, men live and answer to a female figure, and it is believed that they crave this in a partner. The Queen replaces the mother as the authority figure, which is why Female Led Relationships are in demand. It's a win-win situation for you and your man because he will respond to your instruction, and you can be in charge.

CHAPTER 23
Benefits of Men Taking Care of the Household

T oday more men are eager to spend more time at home and take care of domestic duties. Look at any playground during the day and you will see more men with their children as well as out shopping, dining at restaurants, and even going on vacation alone. Women are spending more time devoted to their careers and their men are happy to take up the household duties. There are numerous benefits to men taking care of the household.

Stronger Relationships with Queen

Because mothers are typically seen as the caregiver in a family, it can be especially empowering for males to take on this role. Having success in multiple types of roles can lead to a greater appreciation for the Queen's contributions and a greater appreciation of everything that must be accomplished daily to have a properly functioning household. When men understand the challenges of what was once considered "women's work," they show more empathy and just this understanding can benefit a partnership.

The number one show in 2022 on Netflix was called *Virgin River*. This was a remarkable show due to how all the men were portrayed as being understanding, helpful, and in touch with their emotions. They were all capable of taking care of the household, but they appeared more empathetic toward their wives and girlfriends. This signals a real paradigm shift in society to create a show that mirrors what is happening in our society. Women concentrating on their careers with strong capable yet supportive men taking care of household tasks is the future.

Stronger Relationships with Children

When men are present in the household more, they have more involvement in parenting their children, thus they forge stronger relationships with them. Not only is this beneficial for society as a whole, but positive for families. Studies show that children were found to have positive relationships with both the mother and father when the father stayed at home in a caregiving position while mom focused on her career. Mothers were found to be more connected with their partners, since they had mutual understandings about the pressures of children and work. The empathy your Queen feels when you understand your role and how challenging it is to take care of all household tasks deepens your bond because you are both involved. The Queen makes the rules, and you carry them out and ensure everything runs smoothly.

In contrast to the past, men would leave work and head to the nearest bar or restaurant. They would hang out with friends and leave all household duties and childcare to women. After they became over-exhausted and stressed out, men would be upset when women were not in the mood for sex or connecting, which led to the breakdown of the marriage or relationship. The Female Led Relationship changes this dynamic so that the relationship is successful. When the Queen entrusts the household duties to her capable supportive gentleman, she is less stressed, less overwork, and much happier, which leaves her in a good mood to get turned on for more sex. It's a win-win situation for both of you.

Redefining Social Norms

Redefining social expectations and norms means fathers are perceived as partners in parenting instead of merely bystanders who are called on only in an emergency. Money, career success, and personal achievement are core elements of how we judge a man's manliness and, more or less, his worth. Majority of men who stay at home and take care of the household report feeling inferior to or looked down upon by their male friends who compare salaries, work perks, and promotions. This is largely due to socially accepted norms and patriarchal conditioning. Even when having a father stay home is an overwhelmingly positive choice for everyone involved in the family, research finds the decision still provokes tension and social discrimination. Society, especially in Europe, is slowly normalizing the concept of either parent staying at home.

Stay-at-home dads can help to positively alter perceptions of masculinity, caregiving, and fatherhood. The role of the father becomes stronger in a Female Led Relationship because he bonds more with the children and has a central role in their lives. In the past, fathers were mostly absent, and the breakdown begins when women feel neglected.

The Queen feels ignored and men begin to feel alienated which means they go looking for intimacy elsewhere. Female led relationships completely do a 180 on what are socially accepted norms. Now, a woman's place in the kitchen is replaced by her man, who takes charge of domestic duties. When the baby is crying, men are taking the responsibility of handling it and there is less focus on keeping the status quo set by patriarchal conditioning decades ago. Women focusing on their career and men taking care of the household is normal and acceptable.

Positive Outcomes for Children

While there isn't a lot of research specifically on stay-at-home dads, the American Academy of Pediatrics says that involved fathers have a positive and lasting impact on the health and well-being of their children. Today, there are more stay-at-home dads than ever. Estimates vary, but the numbers have been on the rise for decades. Some recent reports say there are about 7 million men in the United States that act as primary caregiver to their children, with between 2-4 million of them being stay-at-home dads. When dads are more involved with dishes, laundry, cleaning, and other housework, they inspire their daughters to dream bigger and have more ambitious career goals. This also translates into a stronger deeper connection with the Queen who will feel happier and more content seeing the impact on children, particularly girls.

Research shows that children with stay-at-home parents score on average up to six points more than those with both parents working outside the home. The benefits also include emotional well-being. What happens when fathers are absent? Children who grow up with absent fathers can suffer lasting damage. They are more likely to end up in poverty or drop out of school, become addicted to drugs, have a child out of wedlock, or end up in prison.

How does an absent father affect a child? Fatherless children have more difficulties with social adjustment, are more likely to report problems with friendships, and manifest behavior problems. Many develop a swaggering, intimidating persona in an attempt to disguise their underlying fears, resentments, anxieties, and unhappiness.

What are the signs of an absent father? They're dismissive or overwhelmed when the child has an emotional need. They're not interested in the child's interests, friend groups, or schoolwork. They have difficulty expressing their feelings, even with adults. They're unable or unwilling to provide comfort during emotional distress.

Why is a father important to a daughter? A positive father-daughter relationship can have a huge impact on a young girl's life and even determine whether or not she develops into a strong, confident woman. A father's influence in his daughter's life shapes her self-esteem, self-image, confidence, and opinions of men. A dad's involvement in his daughter's life is a crucial ingredient in the development of a young woman's self-esteem. Verbal encouragement, being consistently present in her life, being alert, and sensitive to her feelings, taking time to listen to her thoughts, and taking an active interest in her hobbies are all positive influences from a father figure. Direct involvement and encouragement by her father will help diminish a girl's insecurity and increase her confidence in her own abilities.

As many as 25 percent of children in the U.S. live in households with a mother alone. That is over 18 million children who do not live with a father figure. Additionally, father-only households were noted at just 8 percent.

Researchers have found the absence of fathers has disastrous effects, which include the following:

- **Diminished self-concept and compromised physical and emotional security:** Children consistently report feeling abandoned when their fathers are not involved in their lives, struggling with their emotions, and episodic bouts of self-loathing.

- **Behavioral problems:** Fatherless children have more difficulties with social adjustment, manifest behavior problems, and are more likely to report problems with friendships. Many develop a swaggering, intimidating persona in an attempt to disguise their underlying fears, resentments, anxieties, and unhappiness.

- **Truancy and poor academic performance:** 71 percent of high school dropouts are fatherless. Fatherless children have more trouble academically, scoring poorly on tests of reading, mathematics, and thinking skills. Additionally, children from father-absent homes are more likely to be truant from school, more likely to be excluded from school, more likely to drop out of school at age 16, and less likely to attain academic and professional qualifications in adulthood.

- **Delinquency and youth crime, including violent crime:** 85 percent of youth in prison have an absent father; fatherless children are more likely to offend and go to jail as adults.

- **Promiscuity and teen pregnancy:** Fatherless children are more likely to experience problems with sexual health, including a greater likelihood of having intercourse before the age of 16, foregoing contraception during first intercourse, becoming teenage parents, and contracting a sexually transmitted infection. Many girls manifest an object hunger for males, and in experiencing the emotional loss of their fathers egocentrically as a rejection of them, may become susceptible to exploitation by adult men.

- **Drug and alcohol abuse:** Fatherless children are more likely to smoke, drink alcohol, and abuse drugs in childhood and adulthood.

- **Homelessness:** 90 percent of runaway children have an absent father.

- **Exploitation and abuse:** Fatherless children are at greater risk of suffering physical, emotional, and sexual abuse, being five times more likely to have experienced physical abuse and emotional maltreatment, with a one hundred times higher risk of fatal abuse. A recent study reported that preschoolers not living with both of their biological parents are 40 times more likely to be sexually abused.

- **Physical health problems:** Fatherless children report significantly more psychosomatic health symptoms and illnesses, such as acute and chronic pain, asthma, headaches, and stomachaches.

- **Mental health disorders:** Father-absent children are consistently overrepresented in a wide range of mental health problems, particularly anxiety, depression, and suicide.

- **Life chances:** As adults, fatherless children are more likely to experience unemployment, have low incomes, remain on social assistance, and experience homelessness.

- **Future relationships:** Children with absent fathers tend to enter partnerships earlier, are more likely to divorce, or dissolve their cohabiting unions, and are more likely to have children outside marriage or outside any partnership.

CHAPTER 24
Types of Couples and Female Led Relationships

A variety of couples form different types of Female Led Relationships. Some will be more successful in the long term than others. The four types of couples in dating and relationships are the dramatic couple, conflict-ridden, socially involved couple, and the partner-focused couples. What happens in the daily interaction of each can affect their chances of a successful long-term relationship. Where does Female Led Relationship fit in?

Dramatic Couples

Dramatic couples were more likely to change their level of commitment spontaneously. Their commitment changes with positive and negative events that occur in the relationship. As a result, they make decisions based on the events happening and how they feel, which is why the relationship or marriage can be filled with drama and lots of instability. These types of couples may experience difficulty with setting up the right Female Led Relationship dynamic because there is instability in the power dynamic. Men may not be fully content to serve, and if women are overly dramatic, they may not be able to adequately exert influence over the man and step into their power as Queen. It doesn't mean FLR is impossible, it just means there will be many challenges and conflicts to overcome.

Conflict-Ridden

The commitment in conflict-ridden couples also varies greatly; however, the difference is that these couples will have arguments and disagreements. But they are also more likely to have make-up sex, which brings them back together. Again, there is quite a bit of instability in this type of relationship. Female Led Relationships do not do well with lots of conflict. There is already the assumption that the man has to follow his Queen's lead, but if there is conflict, the disagreements make it very difficult to have a successful FLR. This type of relationship can still have elements of FLR where the woman still wants to be in charge, but enjoying a stable, functioning Female Led Relationship will be more difficult if there is constant conflict.

Socially Involved

Socially involved couples are the ones we see in romantic comedies and are influenced by a network of good friends, family, and co-workers. So, while they can get through issues relying on the help and advice of their network, things can get variable as well as dealing with the pressures of keeping the network happy. Female Led Relationships can thrive with these types of couples as long as the decision is made clear to keep private details of the relationship between the couple.

Friends and family interfering with a relationship is an issue because their views and beliefs may be different from your own and affect your desire to explore female led life in your own way. Couples are often affected by the views of family and friends, and worst yet, if they are in a Female Led Relationship, which goes against social norms. As long as couples make the decision to honor the primary relationship over all others, a Female Led Relationship or female led marriage can be successful long term.

Partner-Focused

Partner-focused couples are those who are very involved with each other and dependent on each other. They are much more aware and able to manage what is happening in the relationship because of a deep bond and connection between the partners. They use what's happening in their relationship to advance their commitment to deeper levels. These types of couples tend to have the best chance of being happy together long term.

Female Led Relationships are successful because they are based on the last type: partner-focused. Since the Queen is focused on her sub and her submissive supportive man is focused on her, there is an overall focus on the relationship. It's easier to fix problems early on and partner-focused couples, such as in Female Led Relationships, tend to maneuver through difficult periods and negative events. This is a significant reason as to why Female Led Relationships are successful and tend to be long-lasting.

CHAPTER 25
What Is Consensual Non-Monogamy?

C onsensual non-monogamy (CNM) involves couples who are married or in long-term relationships but seek to have external sexual encounters with the permission and agreement of their primary partner. So, you and your Queen are married, but you decide to explore mostly casual encounters with others. Consensual non-monogamy encompasses swinging, polyamory, cuckolding, hotwifing, or other types of open relationships. And while consensual non-monogamy has become a hot topic, with examples cropping up everywhere in media, politics, and celebrities, the practice of a couple staying together but seeking outside physical, romantic, or emotional coupling is nothing new.

Four percent of Americans, which is nearly 16 million people, are practicing a non-monogamous style of relationship. Other studies show that over 21 percent of Americans engaged in consensual non-monogamy at some point in their lifetime. Recent studies also found that about

159

one-third of US adults believe that their ideal relationship is non-monogamous to some degree.

Let's face it, we all have sexual fantasies, and sometimes we want to act on them, even when those crushes and fantasies aren't about our partner or spouse. Most of the time, we ignore our fantasies, which can go unfulfilled. For many, cheating is the only option. However, now consensual non-monogamy seems like a better option because there is more honesty and openness, and in many cases, long-term relationships and marriages remain intact. Those who engage in CNM agree on their relationship rules ahead of time, and they allow each other to have romantic and sexual relationships with others.

Thus, CNM differs from monogamy in that there is a firm agreement and open acceptance to have some form of extra outside romantic or sexual relationships. The hit Netflix show *House of Cards* depicted a very solid example of CNM. The character of the First Lady, Claire, was allowed to engage in sex with a younger man, with the firm agreement of her husband, Frank, who was the President. Both people agreed to the sexual encounters.

As for personality, people who seem to engage in CNM tend to have active imaginations, a preference for variety, and a proclivity to engage in new experiences. They held more positive attitudes toward non-monogamy and a greater willingness to engage in these types of open relationships. Does CNM attract people who try to avoid commitment? Studies found that highly avoidant individuals endorsed more positive attitudes toward CNM and were more willing to engage in these types of relationships.

Although avoidant people feel positive about CNM relationships, are they more likely to be in CNM relationships than monogamous relationships? In another study, people in CNM relationships reported lower levels of avoidance compared to people in monogamous relationships. Interestingly, anxiety did not differ between people in CNM and monogamous relationships, and highly anxious people had more negative attitudes toward CNM; however, anxiety was not related to the desire to engage in these types of relationships.

Non-monogamy is growing. People in consensual non-monogamous relationships report relatively high levels of trust, honesty, intimacy, and satisfaction, as well as relatively low levels of jealousy in their relationships. Ethical monogamy was derived from the desire to change non-monogamy from being associated with the negative connotations associated with infidelity and cheating. Will Smith and Jada Pinkett are one celebrity couple of hundreds who publicly spoke about their consensual non-monogamous marriage, and today, they are still happily married. Other celebrities who admitted to enjoying the lifestyle are Gwyneth Paltrow, Jessica Biel, and Thomas Middleditch.

In Female Led Relationships, the decision to pursue consensual non-monogamy is completely up to you and your Queen. It is not mandatory. Many FLR couples are perfectly happy with monogamy where you, the supportive gentleman or her submissive, devote your life to serving one Queen and she is devoted to you. There is no pressure to explore CNM if this is something that will not be beneficial to your lives. While couples in Female Led Relationships can show an interest in consensual non-monogamy, it is not mandatory to create a successful Female Led Relationship or female led marriage. CNM always remains an option for which there must be consent, and both you and your Queen are in agreement about anything you decide to explore together.

CHAPTER 26
Cuckolding and the Female Led Relationship

T he concept of cuckolding and the Female Led Relationship is becoming more popular, and it's becoming one of the most fascinating sexual activities in relationships. There is growing interest in cuckolding from both men and women, even though it is not mandatory to engage in cuckolding as part of a Female Led Relationship. A cuckold is someone who takes pleasure in watching their partner have sex with someone else. There have been many ways in which cuckolding is executed in a relationship, and historically, it was frowned upon since the man would be ridiculed for the assumption that he was unable to perform during sex, leading his partner to seek out another man to satisfy her.

Today, however, cuckolding is much more complex, and this is due to women taking the lead and making the decisions in relationships. Cuckolding is much more than just having sex with another person and requires establishing many rules for everything to go smoothly. I was once a critic of cuckolding since I believed engaging with a third person and introducing them into the relationship would surely cause a rift that would have disastrous consequences. Cuckolding also goes against monogamy, which has been the gold standard for relationships. But at 150,000 searches a month on Google in North America alone, it is growing in popularity.

After investigating the habits of many couples already involved in this lifestyle, I have come to appreciate the reasons why people are obsessed with cuckolding. I also have a much deeper understanding of how it can transform a relationship. Even researchers agree—according to their research, cuckolding couples who act on their desires feel liberated because they can be honest about their sexual fantasies, which leads to more open communication than couples in "normal" relationships. Couples feel closer because there is no hiding or sneaking around.

Today, relationships are dramatically different than they were 20 years ago. The divorce rate is still around 50 percent and infidelity, lying, and dishonesty play a huge role in the destruction of many relationships. But what if this could all change? What if we could be open to our partner's desires and make their happiness our main priority? What if couples could feel completely at ease discussing their needs and wants openly without judgment? Could there be fewer arguments and sneaking around? Could there be more intimacy and sharing, rather than jealousy? I have witnessed couples who have reported a complete turnaround in their relationship when open, honest communication and a willingness to try new things are implemented.

In all industries, change is daunting. What if we never accepted home computers or mobile phones? What if we still needed to talk on the phone instead of texting and there was no social media, just in-person social gatherings? How would our lives be different? The same is true for cuckolding. What was once a major taboo is becoming much more mainstream, and as controversial as it is, cuckolding is here to stay. The only question will be — how does it work in your relationship? This chapter will provide a guide for cuckolding and the rules, which you must follow to be successful. I will also cover how to start cuckolding and how to avoid the common pitfalls. This chapter will also offer the female perspective since, generally, she is in charge and makes the decision of what is right for herself and her man.

If you are a woman interested in adding cuckolding to your current sexual activities, how do you reassure your man and execute it successfully? Maybe you are a man who wants your wife or girlfriend to engage in cuckolding. How do you introduce it? Today, more than 50 percent of couples have a cheating spouse and many end in divorce, so the old ways are not working. Blame new lifestyles, a society that wants instant pleasure, or a change in values. But something has to change. Cuckolding could be an answer to some of the issues leading to infidelity, and there seems to be less lying, deceit, and dishonesty by their lovers and life partners, whether married or in a committed relationship. A relationship that is exciting, loving, honest, and filled with trust should be the new standard.

For me, trust is the most important, rarest, and difficult quality to maintain in a long-term relationship, especially one that involves sex with more than one person. No matter the controversy, cuckolding is here to stay. I will discuss how to engage in it while maintaining a strong bond with your Queen. It is my hope that both men and women will gain tremendous insight into this world, which can lead to safe and happy exploration. This should be an adventure that you experience together with consent from all parties involved.

In the media, cuckolding has become mainstream. In the Emmy-nominated show *Succession* on Netflix, Shiv Roy has her husband sign a contract mutually agreeing she will be having sex with other men. Today, more millennials have admitted to engaging in cuckolding on a regular basis with no issues in the main relationship, and dozens of sites are dedicated to it. Wealthy couples often used cuckolding in which the man was much older than his woman and got to the age when he was unable to perform. In these types of relationships, men often participate in finding their wife's Bull and will watch their sex act.

In my last three books *Love & Obey*, *Real Men Worship Women*, and *Oral Sex for Women*, I focus on the Female Led Relationship where cuckolding is the decision of the woman. She makes the ultimate rule of whether she wants to engage in cuckolding and the man agrees. Even traditionally, cuckolding was initiated by the woman, so I feel that it is mainly a female-dominated realm. With that said, this chapter will focus on cuckolding from the female perspective. However, if you are a man who wants to introduce it to your Queen, this will also help her to get excited since it is a female-driven activity with supportive participation.

In Female Led Relationships, the man's responsibility — under his submission to the female's absolute authority over him — is to allow her freedom, so she can achieve happiness and as much pleasure as possible in her life. Cuckolding, in my opinion, should be approached in a similar manner to the *Love & Obey* philosophy in which the woman is the Queen and her man is the supportive gentleman making all of her fantasies, including cuckolding, come true.

Why is this so important? Because a woman's happiness in a relationship is mandatory. No man can ever exist in a happy relationship without his Goddess also being happy. I have had my share of critics' attempts to argue that my writings are solely for females' control over men; however, the saying, "happy wife, happy life" is true for this very reason.

Whether you are in a Female Led Relationship or not, when the Queen is unhappy, it makes for a very rocky and unsuccessful relationship. FLR cuckolding is the modern style of cuckolding, as the Queen exercises control over her own body, her autonomy from patriarchal and primary male possession, misogynist control, slut- shaming, criticism, and her absolute right to act freely on her emotional and sexual desires as a strong, independent, and powerful woman.

Women are leading in so many ways and exercising their authority more than ever. In 80 percent of the couples I have interviewed, the men agree that they will follow the lead of their women even though it was not formally established that they are in a Female Led Relationship. So, in general, many men welcome the idea of spicing up their relationship with the introduction of a Bull, and they can still participate by watching or being included, depending on the direction of their woman.

For some men, they are turned on by the fantasy of seeing their wife or girlfriend with a man who is more well-endowed or of a different race. In this case, he has to convince his Queen to engage in this type of activity, and it is so much simpler if the woman feels she is in control of the situation. Sometimes cuckolding is used as a form of humiliation—for being the pathetic slave who cannot satisfy his Goddess and must sit quietly while another man satisfies her. So, there are many variations and ways cuckolding can be executed with absolute consent from all three parties.

Relationships can be challenging, and there are numerous cases recently in which couples are looking for ways to spice up the relationship. We all like variety. As women, we love wearing different outfits, shoes, and bags. Men love driving different cars and going to various bars. Some people love being around people of different nationalities or trying different foods—people want variety, and I believe that they need it in their relationships.

As the leader of the female led movement, which was originally frowned upon, I have noticed how receptive people are to this change in power. Men are requesting it, and women are loving it. Many couples are changing the dynamic in relationships because they are looking for variety and ways to fulfill an inner need. There are very few relationships that break up over cuckolding. But 50 percent of traditional marriages still end in divorce. It's a fact that fewer couples in Female Led Relationships divorce. This suggests that even though this is a radical movement, there is something about it that bonds couples.

Research shows that 4 to 5 percent of heterosexual couples have agreed to have an open relationship. In other words, they've given their consent not to be monogamous. The National Opinion Research Center's General Social Survey revealed that more than 20 percent of married men and nearly 15 percent of married women admit to infidelity, a number that's risen almost 40 percent for women in the past 20 years.

In addition, some studies have found that between 30 and 60 percent of married individuals in the United States will engage in adultery at some point in their marriage. So, while only 4 to 5 percent of men and women are choosing to be open about their extramarital relations, somewhere between 15 and 60 percent are opting for a less consensual form of infidelity. Cuckolding is not infidelity, and in general, it is done together with consent.

Cuckolding is transforming relationships, and increased depiction in mainstream media coupled with millions of searches a month online confirms this finding. Research and psychologists have found that when a man or woman sees their partner with someone else, it can excite them and give them feelings of being proud to be with someone who is desired by others. Men and women with attractive partners get this feeling when people are paying lots of attention to their husbands, wives, girlfriends, or boyfriends. Sometimes we all feel good when others want what we have. It's a basic human emotion.

As an extension, realizing your inability to satisfy your partner sexually and be okay with someone else doing it is also exciting and builds a feeling of trust and control because the partner getting cucked is condoning it. Couples often race home to tell their stories and share their experience openly. Some individuals like the humiliation and feeling of subservience. This is true in some Female Led Relationships in which men will be happy when their Goddess is allowed to choose any man she wants. They get turned on by the humiliation they feel when a stronger and more virile man is sexually satisfying his Queen.

Humiliation seems to play a leading role in cuckolding. For some, humiliation ramps up the erotic intensity. Most men are turned on and enjoy watching their partner with someone else. They even love it when their woman laughs or belittles the Bull, who is the additional person introduced into the cuckolding activity. Pleasure also comes from this being the ultimate show of respect to allow your woman to do what she wants.

CHAPTER 27
Cuckolding and Humiliation

C uckolding becomes a significant part of a Female Led Relationship because some men enjoy being subservient and also like the humiliation aspect of the lifestyle. They are turned on by humiliation. Many people relish consensual degradation, and in an FLR, some men find themselves serving their wife and her lover drinks or maybe cleaning the house in the buff while their woman reads on the couch. For these men, the line between eroticism and embarrassment is deeply rewarding.

It's also worth mentioning that humiliation and shame are cousins of guilt. Although there are deep chasms separating these emotions from one another, guilt absolutely plays a role in why some men want a Female Led Relationship. These days, many men are overwhelmed by the benefits they receive every day from male privilege. For a lot of them, the tremendous ease with which they wade through the world contrasts harshly against the ways they know their wife or girlfriend is treated daily by the outside world.

A Female Led Relationship helps them, in some ways, flip the script and reject the notions that have been pushed on them for their entire lives. Often, but not always, Female Led Relationships have strong ties to cuckold culture. The world of cuckolding is bursting with nuance, but a common thread through all styles of cucking is female dominance. The woman in the relationship controls sex, and often has sex with other men.

Depending on the agreement she and her partner reached, she either sleeps with the other men while her husband stays home and cleans. Or she lets her partner watch her get it on with another person. Sometimes, cuckold relationships even entail the man helping the woman pick out her new partners, and he may help her get ready for a date. Drawing her bath, getting her outfit ready, doing her hair, and painting her nails are all common tasks a woman may require of her partner.

Of course, you can have a Female Led Relationship that doesn't involve cuckolding too. Not all people who explore this dynamic feel called to engage in non-monogamy, too. In some situations, a Female Led Relationship simply means the woman is in charge. This still rears its head in the sack in a few different ways. For instance, she may be in charge of initiating sex—either by scheduling it or being the one who decides when it'll happen.

Other reasons for couples wanting cuckolding are to gain excitement from the forbidden. I grew up a very devout Catholic. So much so that I was afraid to steal a pack of gum, much less engage in sex with another man while my partner watched. In my early relationships, I could recall flying into a rage if my boyfriend's eye moved to look at another woman. This jealousy and rigid behavior caused me to become very angry and always worried about cheating.

One of my initial boyfriends suggested an open relationship, and I can recall being so upset about it that I secretly knew we were over. Once I broke out of these restraints based on religious conditioning, I was free to enjoy my relationships. I became less judgmental and more experimental, and I have never regretted a day of delving into this world. It changed my life, my relationship, and my outlook.

Relationships are one of the biggest influences in our lives, which can be a curse every day or a new opportunity to explore and gain more enjoyment and happiness. Once you push those boundaries, you are set free. So, while cuckolding is new, it's growing. I never thought Ashley Madison would become such a large organization spread across hundreds of countries. I realized that there were millions of people searching for new types of relationships. As much as I criticized infidelity, I was open to understanding the trends and changes happening in relationships.

CHAPTER 28
Rules and Boundaries for Cuckolding

C ouples engaging in cuckolding must have rules and boundaries which clearly define what occurs in the relationship, and these must be extended to include the Bull. One of the first rules to establish is where cuckolding will happen. Will it be at your house or the Bull's? Since your comfort is important and safety is mandatory, having it in an environment you all can handle is best. Some couples may choose a hotel room for complete anonymity, which is not a bad choice. You can reserve it and invite the Bull over. Everyone is safe and you are not entering private space.

If this is not an option, you can choose your guest bedroom, ensuring kids are not around. This way it's, again, not in your private space. You can also choose your pool area, if the weather permits, as it's sexy and again allows you to keep your personal areas private. The idea is that since this is a new adventure, keeping it separate from your day-to-day life is recommended.

When you have decided to do cuckolding, it is important to set up clearly defined boundaries with you and your Queen first. How will it play out? Will your Queen approach the Bull, or will both of you? Will the Queen decide how it will play out by giving you instructions, or will you be participating right from the start? This is where a Female Led Relationship is so beneficial because the woman makes the rules.

She decides on what will happen, and all you need to do is follow. So, boundaries must also involve what happens if anyone becomes uncomfortable or wants to stop. It should be clearly established that you will all abort immediately. Getting into arguments of jealous fits of rage should never occur. This keeps everything running smoothly. If your Queen wants to stop, the appropriate and respectful response is to all agree. The Bull's state of mind must also be considered, and if he is unable to perform, you decide on a respectful way to stop. At no time should anyone be made to feel pathetic or bad. You want to prevent any chance of a fun situation spiraling out of control.

Another crucial point in boundaries is to discuss the importance of honesty. The bond between you and your woman must be maintained, and at no time should either of you engage with the Bull alone or without consent. The idea of cuckolding as opposed to cheating is the lying, hiding, and secrecy that often occurs with infidelity. Maintaining trust is the biggest factor. I noticed that in cheating, dishonesty often does the most destruction to relationships, which is why trust and the understanding that both people will always be honest and open about cuckolding is the key. It should be understood that there will be no emotional ties with the Bull from either of you.

These are some of the steps to begin:

1. **Open Communication.** The best place to start is with open communication. Discuss everything very openly. What do you like, and what does she like? How do you see the activity unfolding? What things are completely forbidden? Which areas would you be open to exploring?

2. **Discuss the Fantasy.** The next step is to spend some time talking about the fantasy, so you can explore anything uncomfortable about it. Communication about everything is going to make things so much smoother. Decide on safe words to say if there is anything that feels strange and alarming.

3. **Go Out and Engage with people.** Spend time talking about it or hanging out with others in a bar setting. Without directly engaging a single man, you could set up scenarios to approach a single man in a bar with the goal of merely gaining experience of both of you being comfortable talking with a third. Maybe your Queen wants to dance with another man and flirt with him while you watch. This can be an easy way to determine how you both feel about it.

One of my first experiences with this was when one of my ex-boyfriends encouraged me to dance with a friend of his. At first, I was a bit shocked that he did not care, and I was extremely uncomfortable with the other man aggressively coming onto me in front of my boyfriend who had no issue with it. I later learned that it was something he liked, and he and his friend were used to it. Needless to say, the relationship ended, but what I learned was that dancing and flirting in a scenario like this was enough to determine if cuckolding will be right for you.

If you both cannot get past this step or there are signs of jealousy, you may not be ready. It is important to get comfortable with the process and feel okay if the first time does not go well. After each encounter, even at a bar, discuss your feelings openly. Discuss any hesitations and how it could be improved. Maybe you did not like how she positioned herself with a third and excluded you. Or you like that she took the initiative to approach a man, then invited both of you to sit and chat. It is imperative to discuss everything and ultimately decide if it is worth pursuing. One of my ex-boyfriends asked me to be in an open relationship and I said that I was fine with it, but in reality, I was not ready to pursue anything at the time. My unwillingness to be honest eventually drove a rift between us.

4. **Seek the Bull.** Lots of online dating sites are already set up for cuckolding, with many mainstream ones providing options to explore this. Spend time reviewing profiles and deciding together who would be suitable to join you both. Be respectful when you first approach someone and, again, make the first dates a time to just meet and talk. The more comfortable you are with the Bull—the better the experience will be. Keep personal details to a minimum and make sure everyone is on board with safety and precautions.

5. **Establish rules for the night.** For example, you may say to your partner: "Tonight, let's go out with Dan to

dinner, and afterwards we can come back, go in the hot tub, and just start there." Nothing has to happen. It can just be a night of getting to know him and having fun. Later on, as you get more comfortable, you can have some sensual times in a hot tub with kissing or allowing the Bull to feel her up. The Queen's decision about how far she is willing to go must be established, but there is no harm in starting with baby steps. The more smoothly each encounter goes, the better it is.

Some couples progress with fingering or use of sex toys only as the exploration continues. Then once everyone is on board, you can all plan for the full experience of the Bull having intercourse with your woman while you watch. Some variations can be that perhaps before intercourse, you can have oral sex with your woman, then let her be fucked by the Bull. Whatever happens, she must make the rules, and you can decide if you agree. It's much more fun and inclusive for you to participate in some way, with the main act to be reserved for the woman and the Bull.

Do not feel ashamed if you are feeling jealous. Jealousy is a powerful human emotion. It doesn't mean you're closed-minded or prudish. No matter how "cool" you are, jealousy is going to flare up. That doesn't mean that "this kind of relationship isn't for you." Jealousy typically means you need some special attention. As a partner in a significant relationship with someone, you must be willing to work through your feelings.

Opening yourselves up to new sexual experiences can bring on all sorts of feelings, and you must be allowed to experience them openly. Many couples go through this, and it is perfectly normal. The emotions are part of the thrill ride, the jealousy, the passion, and the desire, which is what makes this so exciting to everyone involved. You both also need to be respectful of the Bull and of any hesitations.

Humans seem to have evolved to be primarily monogamous, with occasional cheating, said University of Michigan psychology professor William McKibbin, PhD. As a result, about 4 percent of children worldwide are fathered by someone other than the man who believes he is the father, according to a meta-analysis published in the *Journal of Epidemiological Community Health* (Vol. 59, No. 9). That tendency allows females to have more genetic variation among their offspring, but for the cuckolded man, not good.

To defend against cuckoldry, men have developed a variety of behavioral and biological defenses, McKibbin said. He also found that men at greater risk for cuckoldry, as measured by the proportion of time they'd spent away from their partners, became more interested in having sex with their partners.

They also found their partners more attractive and engaged in "mate guarding" behavior. This effect was independent of the amount of time since the couple last had sex, so it wasn't just the result of built-up desire — and it was moderated by how much a man trusted his mate not to cheat, McKibbin found. One such finding, in McKibbin's *Comparative Psychology* study, indicates: Men at risk for cuckoldry were later more likely to pressure their partners into having sex. More sex in this case is not always better because it is driven by fear. In this case, the trust factor is also threatened, which could lead to long-term issues.

The First Cuckolding Encounter

Now that all of the discussion, practice, and agreement has happened, it's time to get to your first encounter. This is likely to bring forth a lot of excitement and anticipation. Ensure you are equipped with your safety items: condoms, birth control, etc. You may want to have a set of sheets set aside specifically for this. Even better, if it happens in a hotel room or a place separate from your main home. If you have kids, ensure you do not expose them in any way to this activity.

I recommend setting schedules and choosing a time to meet. It may be a good idea to meet at a restaurant or bar. You should both try to dress to impress in something applicable to the act. Your Queen can also pack extra outfits or sex toys. Personal hygiene is of the utmost importance, which is why a hotel room works so that you have access to a bathroom. If you decide to have it in your home, it might be wise to designate a specific room for it so you can set it up, with the mood and ambiance of your choice. Pools, hot tubs, Jacuzzis, beachfront with access to a beach, or a penthouse suite overlooking the city are all wonderful areas to reserve for the first encounter.

When you first get to the place, start with getting everyone comfortable. Have some drinks and listen to music. You can begin with some light play with your Queen. Just engage slowly and sexy to get everyone in the mood. Then you can all move to the bedroom. If your Queen has decided you will watch, go to your chair and allow her to lead.

She should already have determined how she wants to have intercourse and allow things to unfold naturally. Be open and stick to your established boundaries. No one should go off-script. It may be wise to make the first encounter short. Be aware of how you feel during the first time, so you can decide if cuckolding will happen again in the future. The key is to enjoy the moment. Focus on your Queen and her enjoyment. Refrain from intervening unless she specifically allows you to jump in. Then, only focus your attention on her.

The more comfortable everyone gets, the better things will flow. Once the encounter is over, the Bull can leave, and you and your Queen can continue together, cuddle, or talk. Take showers or just unwind. It is essential to have a period of togetherness after the act.

CHAPTER 29
HotWifing and the Female Led Relationship

Hotwifing is when men get enjoyment from showing off their women and seeing the reaction of other men, but he still prefers to be alpha in the relationship or marriage. In hotwifing, the man derives pleasure from other men enjoying his wife. He may even be adequate and get involved in the sex act with the other man. The husband of a hotwife considers it a compliment to himself that other men desire his wife. He takes pride in having such a hot wife who is sexually charged.

Hotwifing works in Female Led Relationships because it is empowering. Women feel sexy and free from typical societal limitations and can be appreciated by more than one man. Hot wives are in control of their sexuality, and the attention boosts confidence in and outside of the bedroom. Hotwifing is especially great for those with a high sex drive. Some Queens have reported feeling a unique sense of power when in a room full of potential conquests. They know they can have anyone they want without guilt. One Queen describes the thrill of having the experience of another man, flirting with her while her husband sat on the other side of her, looking on. There was no tension, jealousy, and a feeling of complete ease.

Since hotwifing is predominantly a female led activity today, many couples enjoying this lifestyle are already in a Female Led Relationship. The woman will be in charge of the important decisions and carries more authority in the relationship.

The Queen's decision must be respected and followed. The first rule of Female Led Relationships is that sex is for the Queen's pleasure. If you have come to an agreement that it is beneficial for her to interact with the Bull while you watch, then you must adhere to it. Perhaps the Queen decides she wants you to participate, and this is what you will do.

However, clear boundaries must be established for both of you and the outside man. Everything must be clearly explained to the Bull before engaging in anything to prevent unwanted activity. When the Queen decides she wants to make the first move to start things off, this must be respected. Men in a Female Led Relationship must never take it upon themselves to initiate anything with hotwifing not authorized by the Queen. Since she will probably be the person engaging with a stranger, she needs to be careful and confident about how this is done. She must decide what she is comfortable with and what she prefers to avoid.

Hotwifing should always be approached with great care and respect for all people involved. Consent is extremely important. In the Female Led Relationship, the man is the supportive gentleman. You are supporting the Queen's interaction with another man. As part of that support, if she decides she wants you to get involved, then you can do so. Hotwifing needs to be a positive experience for you and your Queen. The idea is that you are both in a Female Led Relationship and are in love. You both want to stay with each other in a long-term relationship.

The Queen successfully and ethically deals with having outside lovers and keeping her primary relationship strong. This is very challenging, so any decisions related to hotwifing must not be taken lightly. One way that you can show your true submission and devotion is in the preparation phase by helping her get ready for the event. Similar to a Queen preparing to attend an event, her helpers assist her in getting ready. When you spend some time assisting your Queen prepare, you reinforce your bond as her supportive gentleman.

Hotwifing can be an exciting part of a Female Led Relationship, because as the supportive gentleman, you are allowing your Queen to do what will make her happy. It can be a very exciting activity for both of you to do together, but you still need to follow the rules of FLR. Sex is for the Queen's pleasure first. You exist to bring the Queen pleasure. With your acceptance and respect throughout the interaction, you show your commitment to her happiness. This means you allow her to lead the interaction and obey her rules. You are respectful of her interaction with the outside man, the Bull, and you adhere to any agreements made. You encourage open communication before and after the act, ensuring you're both fulfilled by the experience.

Men indulge in fantasies every day either through their consumption of porn or during intimate times with their partner. Hotwifing can be the real-life fulfillment of a fantasy.

Many men desire to see their wives engaging in sex with another man after seeing it in a porn video or reading about it. Sometimes it's a fantasy they have had since early adulthood.

Other times, it's more than that. He wants to show his Queen his devotion. He derives sexual satisfaction from knowing he is in service to his woman, and she is still his Queen. The man still feels like he is in control because he wants to see his Queen with a man who is better able to satisfy her and may even be more well-endowed or more muscular, for his own satisfaction. Often, these relationships are in pursuit of fulfilling the husband's or the couple's fantasies. This can apply to any woman whose husband feels she is hot enough to attract another man or for the cuckold in which he is not sexually capable of solely satisfying her. In the world of kinky sex, either form of expression simply means the husband desires some level of interaction between his wife and another man.

While the concept of another man holding, kissing, and making love to your wife is typically considered to be a bit abnormal, it is a fantasy that many men and women have. In fact, research has shown that a majority of men fantasize about watching their wife engage in some degree of sexual activity with another man. Today, many couples consider cuckolding or hotwifing to be fun, exciting, and beneficial to their marriage. It is obvious why women like it since it allows them to fulfill their wildest sexual fantasies. In addition, many couples share this sexual fantasy of taking their relationship to a kinkier level.

Research shows that couples have fantasies about hotwifing, but many are afraid to express themselves because they fear what their partner might think of them. So, one of the benefits of acting on a hotwifing fantasy is the real-life fulfillment of your most secret desire. It also provides women with a newfound modern freedom and the right for her to choose what she does with her body. Modern women do not want to be controlled by a man.

In female led marriage, women have the right to do as they see fit. The wife gets the freedom to enjoy the company of the opposite sex. Many women in female led marriages enjoy the company of men other than their husbands. They practice the idea that modern women are "not the property of their husbands." This modern way is allowing women to have the chance to enjoy life more. When a man allows his woman to be in the company of other men, she enjoys a refreshing kind of intimacy and freedom with all her men, including her husband.

In female led marriage, women are freed from the jealousy of their husbands. Jealousy is one of the major reasons many relationships fail. Jealousy arises from male ego concerns and male insecurities. This male ego-based jealousy is a contributing factor in many disagreements and breakups. As we learned, jealousy comes from ancient genetic coding in men to protect their future lineage by making sure that his wife's offspring are his as well. Hotwifing is a modern experience involving birth control, which can help to rid the man of his feelings of jealousy. In a female led marriage, the wife can enjoy her freedom to be who she wants to be. She knows her husband will be obedient, and he will have her best interests and her pleasure at heart, which helps her trust him more and enjoy the marriage.

Relationships are built on trust and communication. Hotwifing can increase trust and communication within relationships. If you want to be truly happy, with a lasting relationship, you must ensure that you understand each other and give one another the chance and freedom to be who you genuinely are, including living out your most secret fantasies. Before you begin to dive into actual hotwifing or cuckolding, you both need to agree with each other about your intent to participate. The women in Female Led Relationships are typically sexually dominant, while the man takes on a more submissive role, only becoming involved with her sexually or with her lover when the wife permits him to. Sometimes the man will remain in chastity and completely celibate for the entire marriage.

As a man, you may feel that you are with the hottest woman on earth, and it's every man's desire to have a woman who is another man's dream. Hotwifing gives a man the perfect chance to allow other men to appreciate how beautiful and desirable his woman is, which typically serves to increase both his love and respect for her. It boosts both the man and the woman's confidence. In female led marriages and both cuckolding and hotwifing experiences, women have a chance to express themselves. When a woman knows she has the support of her man to do whatever she desires, she feels great about herself, which helps to boost her own self-confidence. This kind of open and honest relationship increases trust and communication between the couple and brings them closer together.

It is well known that Female Led Relationships increase intimacy. Hotwifing gives a couple the perfect chance to gain important knowledge about themselves and each other that can help heighten their level of closeness and connection. The new sexual adventures and the wide variety of options dramatically deepens a couple's bond. It provides a greater sense of sexual satisfaction for both husband and wife.

Hotwifing creates a lifestyle for attaining physical satisfaction. The woman can spend quality time with men who interest her, which quenches her thirst that otherwise would typically lead to affairs and betrayals in more traditional marriages that destroy trust and relationships. One of the main benefits of Female Led Relationships is that the couple stays together because they are far more open, honest, intimate, loving, and fulfilling than many people think.

CHAPTER 30
Polyamory

People often confuse cuckolding with polyamory, but they are different. A polyamorous relationship from the Greek word *poly*, meaning "many," and Latin *amor*, meaning "love," is a non-monogamous relationship. Polyamory occurs in a Female Led Relationship when a couple wants to have intimacy with multiple partners all the time, and it is an actual lifestyle. Many celebrities have admitted to engaging in polyamory. Miley Cyrus, as an example, made polyamory famous when she revealed that even though she was married, she is openly polyamorous. What was even more shocking was that Miley indicated her partners can be men women, gay, straight, or transgender.

Although polyamorous couples have the freedom to be non-monogamous, there are still rules laid out that must be followed. A great example of this was in the movie *Savages*. All three characters lived together, and each man had sex with the main female character Ophelia, played by Blake Lively. Even the Mexican cartel characters criticized this type of living as "savage" compared to their way of killing and murdering associates in the cartel. The irony is pervasive in this movie, but it was a good portrayal of modern polyamory. The three were considered the family unit.

Cuckolding is not the same. While the Queen has sex with a Bull, he is not part of the main family unit, and in general, cuckolding is not happening with a gay man or a transgender. Cuckolding is mainly about sex or humiliation, but it does not involve living and inviting others into the family unit. Polyamory may be the choice of some couples, but as Miley discovered, it's not simple. Her polyamorous ways were not shared by her husband Liam Hemsworth, which led to their separation and divorce earlier in 2020. Their split also highlighted an extremely important point in that both the man and woman in the relationship must be on board with the lifestyle, otherwise, there will be a great deal of conflict.

I also personally feel that while cuckolding appears to be much more restrained and selective while retaining a strong bond in the main relationship, inviting and living with several people as part of the family unit represents a much more complicated situation to manage. Cuckolding or hotwifing can be one or two nights of fun, whereas polyamory often involves living with multiple people on a day-to-day basis. Two completely different scenarios not to be confused.

Polyamory is also growing out of economics and a shortage of straight men. Since it can be extremely expensive to live in a city, now a couple can invite a third or multiple people to live in their home, and this can lead to polyamory where they are also engaging in sex. There are numerous examples of polyamorous couples having children and living as a happy family unit. The important part is managing the relationship among all who participate and encouraging open communication and consent. In the Netflix series *Narcos*, the boss of the Cali Cartel had three women he engaged with, and they all lived together happily, but his schedule with each had to be managed.

Polyamory becomes even more complicated in a Female Led Relationship as there must still be a Queen in charge of the household and her submissive man. If there is an extra man or woman, you must decide how he or she will fit into the FLR dynamic. There must also be clear rules as to what happens in daily life and what will be the power dynamic. It's not impossible, but there are many challenges and issues to discuss and obstacles to overcome. Children as part of polyamory and Female Led Relationships also must be managed properly to understand not only the female led dynamic but multiple relationships as part of the family unit.

CHAPTER 31
Swingers Lifestyle and Female Led Relationship

W hat's the most exciting time in life? Is it the first kiss? Dating and searching for a partner? Why is it so exciting? Is it the flirtation, suspense, and excitement of the unknown? What's going to happen during or after the date? These are the aspects missing from a long-term relationship, and if we are being honest with ourselves, we miss these moments.

So, how do you rekindle some excitement and adventure in a long-term relationship or marriage? Start dating again and meeting new people. Enter swinging and the friends with benefits lifestyle. There are more media coverage, movies, and Netflix shows coming out today on the subject than ever before. Google logs 600,000 searches a month for the terms "swinging" and "friends with benefits," and several clubs, social events, and vacations are available for those interested in swinging.

Katy Perry's song "I Kissed a Girl" propelled girl-on-girl experimentation into the mainstream. All of a sudden, trying it out was suddenly popular, and this is the sentiment of many couples who remain together but decide to add the experimentation and exploration of swinging into their marriages and long-term relationships. Today, women have been found to initiate swinging more often, and they are using it as an opportunity to explore their own desires. Men are loving this as they fulfill their ultimate fantasies of threesomes and multiple partners. Swinging is becoming female led and dramatically changing things. Swinging typically refers to couples switching sexual partners with other couples, but "the lifestyle" encompasses people looking to have recreational sex or sexual experiences with anyone outside of the relationship. This might include inviting a third party for a threesome or attending sex-positive clubs or parties.

The urban dictionary describes swinging as a lifestyle of non-monogamy where sexual relations occur outside the established couple. Swingers are people who feel the need to explore and get satisfaction from others outside the primary partner. It is generally only successful when both partners engage in it with other couples, and there is complete trust and security in the relationship.

Considered part of the alternative lifestyle, swinging was often frowned upon and shunned by normal society. It was believed to be in the same realm as cheating and infidelity, but swinging couples report more happiness by following this lifestyle and generally do not get divorced. With swinging, there is no cheating, lying, and sneaking around, which often leads to trust issues. Instead, couples enjoy the night or weekend that they devote to meeting other couples, and any exploration is done with complete consent from all those involved.

Swinging is often considered safer than dating because you are not meeting strangers alone, and though there is sexual fun, swinging often leads to long-term friendships. For many, an advantage is the increased quality, quantity, and frequency of sex. Some people engage in swinging to add variety to their otherwise conventional sex lives or for curiosity. Some couples perceive swinging as a healthy outlet and means to strengthen their relationship. Others regard such activities as merely social and recreational interaction with others. Researchers estimate that 40-50 percent of all first marriages will end in divorce or permanent separation, and about 60-65 percent of second marriages will end in divorce. Although divorce has always been a part of American society, divorce has become more common in the last 50 years. Yet swingers rarely get divorced.

Swinging involves both partners in a committed relationship sexually engaging with others for entertainment purposes and building new friendships "with benefits." Most couples in traditional conservative "patriarchal" relationships get into a "sexual rut," and where's the fun in that? A "sexual rut" is the worst rut of all because it robs you of intimacy. Swinging allows for a whole different life experience and a whole new wild world where your sexual fantasies can come true. You can escape the monotony and boredom and learn from others, hang around with fun-loving people, and of course, expand the sexual scenarios you're willing to experience with your partner.

What you must understand is that an open relationship cannot exist without openly communicating with each other.

Keeping secrets and deceiving your partner about your sexual desires, needs, and activities will eventually become toxic and create feelings of neglect, insecurity, rejection, jealousy, and betrayal—all of which are sure to destroy your marriage or relationship. But this does not have to be the case. Many couples have reported the opposite. They spend more time together; as a result, they are more relaxed, happier, and sexually fulfilled.

In the swinging world, couples make their own rules around what they need within relationships and marriages and agree to abide by the boundaries they set. Couples who select this type of lifestyle seek one or many partners for the pure excitement of getting what they don't receive sexually from their primary relationship. But the primary relationship is maintained as most important, and each couple decides what is allowed and not allowed.

Swingers will often have lasting friendships with others of the opposite sex while enjoying sexual pleasures from them as well. Things never get stale, and it usually spices up the bedroom. Some couples enjoy watching other couples. They learn new tricks and techniques, and they are free to explore. After years of being together, without a lot of effort, it is almost impossible to experience the excitement and jitters you felt when you were first dating. Many dead marriages come alive when both people are free to explore their ultimate fantasies without lying, sneaking around, or cheating. And you are doing it together, which only serves to strengthen your relationship.

Women can approach swinging differently from men. Some want to experiment with women, while others need more arousal than they feel is possible with their men. Many are bi-curious, and rather than keeping these feelings bottled up inside, getting depressed, and numbing their feelings with wine every night, they are free to explore their sexuality and fantasies. Men also get the excitement and adventure they crave.

Swinging also happens with same-sex couples and is very popular with gay men. Most swingers feel that it brings more joy and fulfillment into their lives and enriches their marriages. However, they admit that swinging will not fill a void in their marriage, and this is where negative experiences can occur. Swinging will not fix a broken relationship, and if this is where you and your partner are at, you must seek the advice of a therapist.

CHAPTER 32
Obedience in Female led Relationships

The role of obedience in Female Led Relationships is key to creating a hierarchy of power. Obedience is a form of social influence where an individual acts in response to a direct order from another individual, who is usually an authority figure. It is assumed that without such an order, the person would not have acted in any particular way. Following commands is an essential requirement in a Female Led Relationship. A command given by the Queen to the gentleman is a demand for them to follow without thinking or disobeying.

Why is this important? Because orders instill discipline. Orders are passed from the *Love & Obey* Mistress to the submissive man as a way of ensuring they are both on the same page. Obedience is the following of orders and plays the role of maintaining structure in the Female Led Relationship. Leadership entails commanding respect and a predictable response from the obedient man. Queens must demonstrate they have the capacity to lead others, and they show this by their ability to successfully complete tasks.

For example, graduating from high school, college, graduate school, or working successfully in a career or as a professional. To be a *Love & Obey* Queen, a woman should demonstrate that she can run, manage, and maintain order in her relationship. As I mentioned earlier, most women who desire FLR are well-educated and smart. Often, they are better educated and smarter than their man, so this is not usually an issue.

Obedience is nothing new in society and in our interpersonal relationships. So, it's not surprising that it plays a key role in a Female Led Relationship. Many traditional cultures regard obedience as a virtue; historically, societies have expected children to obey their elders. Throughout time, slaves had to obey their owners in colonial America. Similarly, serfs obeyed their lords and kings in feudal society, and people complied with their God. Compare the religious ideal of surrender and its importance in Islam. The word Islam literally means "surrender."

In some Christian weddings, obedience is formally included along with honor and love as part of a conventional bride's but not the bridegroom's wedding vow. In a Female Led Relationship, it is the opposite, the man vows obedience but the *Love & Obey* Mistress only promises to lead and command. As a man, you must obey your superior woman, calling her Goddess, Queen, or Mistress. You should behave obediently as a child does with his mother, and if you do good, you will not have to fear any frightening punishment. Whatever your woman says to you, do as she tells you, because, through her, you will win her love and achieve happiness.

Obedience is required when your female authority figure instructs you to do something. Whereas traditional male-female roles are determined by conformity to social pressures and adhering to the norms of the majority. Obedience involves a hierarchy of power and status. The person giving the order, the *Love & Obey* Mistress, has a higher status in the relationship than the person receiving the order, the obedient gentleman. This higher status creates order, calm, and a nurturing loving environment.

Obedience is the act of following orders without question because they come from an authority you have accepted. There are many legitimate authorities in a person's life, from parents to teachers to law enforcement and even spiritual and government leaders. Most of these authority figures mentioned above are given their authority by society. We are just told to follow what they tell us to do. In other words, we are trained to be obedient to these people. Every person at some time in their life has followed a superior without questioning why they are doing what they are doing.

For example, we never question why we take tests in school. We just take them because we are told to do so. We never question a lot of the rules that people say "are in our best interest" because they are usually told to us by someone that is in a position higher than us. In the Female Led Relationship, the woman is granted the highest position of authority and the man agrees to obey her. In exchange, he earns the right to live in a safe, loving, and compassionate female led lifestyle.

Chaos is a situation of confusion and a disorderly state, lacking leadership. With an accepted authority figure and strict obedience, any guesswork on what to do goes away and reduces anxiety on how to respond in various situations. The concept of a loving female authority gives your woman control over you and your obedience is expected. Her orders and your obedience determine the positions of power that define each of your roles. Once you accept your woman as your Mistress, and she accepts you as her obedient gentleman, you will see that you have eliminated elements of presumption, confusion, and incidents of confusion.

Additionally, orders establish control of various situations. Hearing your Mistress's commands, you take action immediately and you follow her orders. This behavior pattern eliminates instances of second-guessing, wrong decisions, fear, and failure to follow her preferred course of action. This predictable behavior pattern also helps prevent any breakdown in communication. Following your Queen's commands upholds the chain of authority. In every human institution, individuals follow a particular existing hierarchy, from the superiors to the junior staff.

In the military, for instance, the chain of command defines its leadership system. In the military, everyone has a rank and there is a chain of command. Within corporations, people have positions and jobs, from the lowest with no authority to the highest person in charge of the corporation's plan of action. It is the same in a Female Led Relationship. The failure to follow orders appears as disrespect to the Queen, which is an offense that requires punishment. She may not necessarily ask or give a clear order, but the submissive man is obliged nevertheless to obey.

Moreover, since the obedient man takes command before beginning any task, he promises to uphold the desires of the female by showing allegiance to her as his rightful leader and following her orders. The Female Led Relationship structure emphasizes the values and principles of discipline and respect for the Queen who has absolute authority. To portray these values, gentlemen have to obey and follow orders given, as they work toward achieving the female's life goals. Only with your obedience can you maintain a loving Female Led Relationship.

CHAPTER 33
Spanking and Female Led Relationships

While BDSM and spanking are not a requirement in Female Led Relationships, many couples want to add many aspects of domination and submission into their sex lives. Why is the fantasy of spanking so exciting? Men and women have both admitted to having fantasies of being tied up and whipped. More couples have admitted to engaging in spanking and adding it to their sex lives.

I can recall the number of times men begged me to spank them in bed. Being a strong, fully capable woman, they were excited at the thought of being under my control, and I was fully physically capable of administering a very heavy-handed spanking that could bring even the biggest, aggressive man to tears. I could see how spanking could spice up any sex life and how it led to some very interesting and adventurous lovemaking. Men became obsessed and many of them need it to feel fully under their woman's control.

In a Female Led Relationship, the desire to be controlled by a strong female becomes even more important. More women are taking control of many aspects of their lives, and many are leading countries, governments, corporations, cities, households, and now the bedroom. My previous books *Love & Obey* and *Real Men Worship Women* are blockbuster hits and provide the essential guidance that a couple needs to build a lasting, successful relationship. Part of keeping the spark alive in all relationships is to add discipline. Relationship discipline takes spanking to a whole new level in the sex life, and a better sex life naturally means a better relationship in many cases.

Why has spanking become so popular? Our desire to engage in spanking comes out of our need for attention. The only time most children get attention is when their parents are disciplining them, and maybe as adults we crave this undivided attention. Though spanking children is not advisable and outlawed, spanking in the bedroom has skyrocketed. As the leader of the *Love & Obey* and Female Led Relationship movement, I have seen how spanking has particularly become popular with women spanking men. So, I will be exploring spanking as it pertains to fun displays of discipline and dominance in the relationship.

Though spanking comes out of BDSM, this book is in no way intended to instruct on the particular practices or customs of BDSM. Here, we focus on fun things the Queen can do to discipline her man in a playful respectful way if the man desires it and there is full consent. I will also touch lightly on spanking as a means of serious discipline for those couples who wish to learn more about this and, of course, how spanking can be added to as part of relationship discipline. Overall, spanking during sex is meant to add some variety and that element of fun and adventure to any relationship.

During one of the first parties I've ever attended for fetish, a massive gathering with thousands of people were moving through a maze of different rooms set up with everything to do with BDSM, bondage, and torture. It was straight out of the movie *Eyes Wide Shut*. In one room, I observed an old man getting saran wrapped and strung up, hanging from the rafters. Three dominatrixes prepared themselves like a scene out of the movie *Wonder Woman* on the island of Themyscira when the female warriors were preparing for battle. Then once they were armed with their floggers, they began to flog the man while we all watched. But what I cannot stop thinking about was the smile on his face. He urged them to beat him harder and more.

They would replace their floggers for riding crops, and no matter how hard they whipped the man, he got happier and seemed to be in a state of ecstasy. This got me thinking about the idea of spanking in the bedroom and how both the fear of what it could be, and the painful sensations wake up something primal in both men and women. Something which cannot be achieved with any other sexual act. Men who want to be dominated are intensely turned on and the women derive a great deal of satisfaction from completely controlling her man.

Think of the intense excitement you will feel when your Queen ties you up, teases you to death with role-playing, ticklers, and light strokes of a whip. For some, this is a way of life. I know many couples who cannot wait to engage in some kind of dominance play and relationship discipline. Women have admitted to me the satisfaction they get when they can control their men, spank them whenever they want, and they have them begging for more and treating them infinitely better than before.

Spanking can cause many of our deep desires for complete attention from our partners, because let's face it, you need complete, undivided attention when administering and receiving a spanking. It resolves many of the disrespectful behaviors that have arisen and are accepted by society as normal, but which can lead to the unraveling and the eventual destruction of the relationship. How many times have I seen couples spending quality time together and they are on their phones or social media? Spanking in the bedroom is the one time a couple's minds do not wander, and you can't be on the phone. To partake in spanking and relationship discipline, there cannot be distractions, and this is one of the advantages of the relationship.

Within the world of dominance and submission, discipline is often eroticized and executed in a way society wouldn't otherwise condone. But many couples are waking up a dead sex life with the addition of spanking and light BDSM.

In the Female Led Relationships, more men have admitted that they enjoy and have a strong desire for their women to whip them and be aggressive. Hence, this chapter will deal with erotic spanking and how the Queen can administer this discipline to her man during sex. Today, more relationships are being led by women. Women are taking charge in the household and in the bedroom. Men are loving the experience of being under the spell, and the dominance of women and spanking just adds to the feeling of control for the Queen. When women feel empowered, they are at their best and men get excited when they take charge and show their power. So, it's a win-win for most.

205

The popularity of spanking shows no signs of slowing down. Spanking is fast becoming the favorite bedroom pastime and at 670,000 searches a month, its popularity worldwide is only growing. A recent survey showed that 75 percent of women and 66 percent of men enjoyed erotic spanking. This chapter will serve as an introduction to erotic spanking and provide some fun ideas on how to add spanking to your sexual routine in a safe way. It cannot be understated that safety is the key as well as consent. This must always be a pastime between consenting adults who are in a committed relationship. Added to an already healthy sex life, spanking can be a fun way to spice up the bedroom while fulfilling your fantasies.

When a couple begins a female led lifestyle, they need to discuss how they want to go about it. Are they going to agree on a list of rules first, or will they agree that the female leader will train the man as she sees fit? Some couples prefer the former while others prefer the latter. Each individual couple must figure out what works for them. In my first book, *Love & Obey*, I used positive reinforcement behavioral training to encourage good behavior, and I do not endorse the use of non-consensual, physical punishment. Today, I still only endorse safe physical punishment, which is consensual and not harmful in any lasting or serious way. A couple must always fully agree before engaging in this practice and both should be adults.

I have come to see why spanking, paddling, whipping, and caning are important and popular erotic forms of training men, especially in a Female Led Relationship. Obedience must be demanded by the Queen if she wishes to rule over each man. A Female Led Relationship may start out as a male sexual fantasy, but it must evolve into a real lifestyle in which the woman leads, and the man obeys, or it simply will not work. Spanking and relationship discipline has the ability to be a fun pastime to your sexual routine, or it has the power to transform the relationship and increase intimacy and respect.

Today, particularly in the bedroom, the tides are turning, and Queens are spanking the men. There is growing interest in spanking as more and more couples are engaging in it. Sex expert Sienna Sinclaire says, "Erotic spanking is all about spanking someone for sexual pleasure for both parties." The person being spanked enjoys it, and the person doing the spanking also gets enjoyment. Spanking has become so popular that there are now thousands of products available on Amazon to ensure you can create the perfect spanking experience. But is spanking during sex a new concept? Apparently not.

Today, in Female Led Relationships, many men enjoy being spanked by their Queen, and many have introduced it as an acceptable weekly—even daily—occurrence. Learning proper techniques and ways to introduce it into the sex life is key. I will be discussing all aspects of erotic spanking, including the history, proper techniques, tools, and much more. The goal of this book is to help men and women engage in fun, healthy, safe, and consensual spanking as part of their sex routine. I will also add some information on the serious practice of relationship discipline, and I will touch lightly on BDSM.

It is my wish that all couples use this to build more intimacy and spice up your sex life. A healthy, fun sex life can dramatically change your relationship for the better. Spanking is a pivotal part of the Female Led Relationship where the woman administers the spanking both for fun times as well as discipline. Being the leader of the *Love & Obey* movement, which promotes a healthy and safe female led lifestyle, I believe spanking with consent from both the Queen and her man fits perfectly into the female led world. Women are already in charge and more than capable of giving a great spanking session. So why is spanking growing, and why is it such a turn-on? Men have been known to crave fantasies of being dominated and women love powerful men. Spanking has the power to transform a relationship from dull, boring, monotonous, and failing to exciting, intimate, and rewarding. Happy safe spanking.

According to a study published in the Journal *Social Psychological and Personality Science* by Joris Lammers and Roland Imhoff, social power reduces inhibition. In other words, powerful, wealthy men are aroused by being dominated by women in bed. In one of the earliest episodes of the show *Game of Thrones*, Khaleesi — after taking it from her husband played by Jason Momoa — is instructed to dominate him. Once she does this, she is treated like a Queen and a Goddess.

But another study claims that power frees people from their inhibitions, and thereby increases sadomasochistic thoughts in everyone, masochistic tendencies in men who are being hurt or tortured, and sadistic thoughts in women. So, this is the reason why men crave torture and get turned on when aggressive women do this, particularly during sex.

The findings of the study showed that power increases the arousal to sadomasochism. Furthermore, the effect of power on arousal by sadistic thoughts is stronger among women than men, while the effect of power on arousal by masochistic thoughts is stronger among men than women. Masochism is defined as deriving sexual gratification from one's own pain or humiliation. As was uncovered, men crave physical torture from dominant women, which coincides with my findings as well. Men love the pain felt when a powerful woman smacks them on the behind, and the powerful woman is turned on by doing the act.

A 2013 study found that both dominant and submissive practitioners of BDSM were less neurotic, more extroverted, more open to new experiences, more conscientious, and less sensitive to rejection. They also had higher subjective well-being compared to the control group. This could mean two things: People with these traits are attracted to kinky sex, or kinky sex can help you grow and gain confidence.

I always think of the scene from *The Wolf of Wall Street* where Jordan Belfort is so taken with his dominatrix Venice that he was caught calling out her name in his sleep. In the scene, Venice's preferred punishment is to pour candle wax on his butt while whipping him, and he enjoys it so much that he is dreaming about it. But Mr. Belfort, a powerful head of an investment firm, craves this activity despite having access to thousands of women from all walks of life in various sexual escapades, and yet this is the one he dreams about.

There are many reasons why erotic spanking is exciting. First, there's the physical sensation. If done properly, spanking stimulates a person's genitals indirectly and creates a subtle sensation that is, no doubt, pleasurable. On the other hand, there's the psychological aspect of it. Erotic spanking can also have a lot to do with role-playing and pretend-punishment that flares up one's imagination and makes the sexual experience much more intense.

BDSM (which stands for bondage and discipline, dominance and submission, and sadism and masochism) and spanking can allow people to begin experiencing this practice in a fun way. Spanking comes out of BDSM. Discipline in BDSM is the practice in which the dominant sets rules that the submissive is expected to obey. When rules of expected behaviors are broken, punishment is often used as a means of disciplining. In BDSM, rules can be made so that a submissive or sub knows how they should behave so that the dominant is not displeased.

In Female Led Relationships, this translates into men behaving properly according to the rules of the Queen. Rules can also be for reminding subs of their inferior status, or for training a novice sub. In BDSM, when such rules are broken, punishment is often used as a means of discipline. Punishment itself can be physical such as caning, or psychological such as public humiliation, or a combination of both through bondage and spanking. So, spanking during sex extends from this practice of BDSM and discipline, which becomes a fun way for the Queen to exert her dominance over her man for both of their enjoyment.

What turns on one person about spanking is personal. Shelby Devlin, a sex and intimacy coach, says that the person getting spanked may love the feeling of powerlessness, while another person might only be about the physical sensation. So, when you first decide you want to explore spanking, she may suggest taking time out for self-reflection. What is it about spanking that turns you and your partner on? Analyze it and discuss it.

Dawn Michael, a certified sexuality counselor and marriage and family therapist with a PhD in human sexuality, says that being submissive or dominant with your partner can be a sexy role-play that spanking easily falls under. She says that "spanking can be a turn-on for both a man and a woman who enjoy being submissive to their partner, working it into a role of submission to their Dom for a man or their master for a woman."

Men have always loved aggressive women and spanking in sex offers the opportunity for women to take control and spice things up during sex. Imagine an entire foreplay session in which she ties you up, blindfolds you, throws you down on the bed, and runs her flogger or horse whip all the way up from your toes to your head, then gives you a few slaps. Afterward, she gets on top and rides you to orgasm. Who can resist?

Almost everyone has some secret desire, fantasy, or fetish that turns them on in the bedroom or elsewhere. Some choose to keep their fantasies to themselves and think about them when they're alone. They consider this part of their sexuality not necessary to share. However, others have a strong urge to share their fantasy or fetish, desiring to act it out with partners. Feelings of guilt, shame, and confusion about our fantasies and what turns us on are common in our society.

What is often difficult for people to understand is that sexual awakening happens when we are children. Although childhood sexuality is a natural part of development, it is often ignored in our culture, shunned, or brushed under the rug as wrong. The child is made to feel ashamed or guilty for having sexual thoughts and desires. No explanations are given, and nothing is talked about.

Women in Female Led Relationships love to give a good spanking to their men. Here's why: In spanking, there is a power exchange, and in a Female Led Relationship, the Queen is in charge. She has the power and the opportunity to exert her power on her man during sex with a little spanking. This can be a great turn-on for both men and women. Also, let's face it—dominance is sexy. Dominance during sex intensifies sexual drive, and powerful women drive men crazy. A woman in a position of power is the desire of every man, particularly to the man who has dedicated his life to serving.

Men are already submissive in a Female Led Relationship, so they have already agreed to their Queen having free reign over them. During sex, heightened levels of sexual pleasure begin once the woman assumes this role of dominance and even suggests spanking. Asserting your authority as a woman during sex portrays to the man that she knows what she wants and is going to have it. This makes her man eager to please and submit. It adds an element of adventure and fear, which can be extremely arousing.

It is normal for sex in long-term relationships to get monotonous and repetitive, so spanking shakes things up and allows the Queen to have the control, which is her deepest desire. I feel that spanking appeals to the deepest of desires of a female led woman, which is to have complete power over her man. Just as children get tired of their old toys, adults also get bored and tired of carrying out the same repetitive sexual routine and styles without the introduction of something new or adventurous.

Spanking adds extra spice by bringing diversification to a regular sexual ritual. Spanking can make things very intimate as the Queen is in total control and the man is vulnerable in assuming positions for her to spank him. Spanking brings about freshly ignited feelings that come with trying a different experience from the norm. This creates intimacy and transports you both to a whole new world and bonds you both in ways you never expected. Agreeing to introduce spanking to your sexual life is an intimate moment built. Carrying out the act together amplifies the bonding.

Many men have testified to feeling great when they get a good spanking from their Queen. A certain stimulus is ignited when a man gets spanked because this triggers the dopamine receptors into action, bringing about sexual pleasure and is an exciting time for both partners. It is important to not engage in kink shaming, which literally means the shaming of another person for their sexual fantasies, which may happen occasionally.

Even the most compatible partners can have wildly different sexual preferences. In any sexual relationship, you're bound to be turned on by different things. That's why it's best to be kind about it when your partner tells you something they want to try in bed, even if it's not for you. Sexual fantasies are best shared as part of "dirty talk" during sex. Others may feel more comfortable bringing up the topic during more neutral times when sex isn't on the table.

A psychologist and certified sex therapist advised the following: Create a safe space in which you're not in overwhelmed work mode, face each other, and have eye contact. Let them know that this might be difficult for you or that you've been waiting for the right moment. It's also usually easier to share something with others once you've become okay with it yourself, so if this is a kink you carry unneeded shame over, it might be good to work through that shame with a sex therapist or in your own time before discussing with a partner. Additionally, it's important to remember that as long as your fantasy is between two consenting adults, it's likely to be completely normal.

A female led lifestyle involves setting up some rules for a man's behavior that his Queen can monitor. If he breaks a rule, then he must be disciplined for doing so. This discipline teaches men to behave in a more submissive, obedient, and loving way. Some couples set up rules together, while others rely on the Queen alone to create them. Some rules may be suggested by the man since he wants to work on some negative aspect of his own behavior or attitudes that he believes is holding him back from becoming a more submissive and loving man.

Some couples write down the rules, while others are quite happy to keep them on a purely verbal basis of agreement. Some men may tend to debate the Queen's rules when they are called out for breaking them. This is not considered good behavior and can be disrespectful to the Queen. The most important point is consistency. If you both as a couple decide that light spanking be used when the man misbehaves, then the Queen must follow through with the spanking, and the man must obey.

Inconsistent rules are not normally a huge problem in female led households. The Queen cannot be unreasonable, but if it is agreed on, then both must follow through. Many couples find it simple and straightforward to agree on a consistent set of rules for his behavior. These rules may change and develop over time. They may be added or subtracted, as needed and common sense dictates. A Queen must create consistent consequences for his man's unruly behavior. This simply means that a Queen may spank a man briefly for a minor offense, but she may whip a man to tears for a more serious offense, ensuring that he is sobbing repentantly by the end of his punishment.

The amount and severity of the actual spanking varies because the Queen may need to adjust these based on the man's attitude, but the relative outcomes must be consistent. Light spanking for a very minor offense, and heavy paddling with tears for a more serious offense. The consequence of a man's different types of bad behavior must be consistent, even if they are not identical. Delivering consistent consequences for male bad behavior is about maintaining the relative differences between offenses so that the reason for the punishment based on the seriousness of his bad behavior is always clear. He should know that if he gets a light spanking for an insignificant offense, he will get a severe whipping for a serious offense.

CHAPTER 34
Transition from Patriarchy to Female Led Relationships

One of the biggest issues that arises in relationships is the transition from Patriarchy to Female Led. How can men learn to do something if they feel it may go against their nature? You've been taught to take control and "be a man," be strong and assertive all of your life, and now, with times changing and a desire to serve your Queen, you must adapt and change. I recognized a long time ago that real change in relationships can be the most difficult undertaking. Even therapy without practicing the principles learned can result in failure.

Have you ever come across a strong woman who seemed perfect relationship material but after a few dates it's apparent you didn't feel the same level of attraction as you originally felt for her? And you wanted to take things to the next level, but for some reason, you can't seem to show a similar intention and you didn't know what to do about it? Or do you often struggle to keep her interest for long? Have you ever slept with a woman too soon only to realize that she has almost disappeared from your life for no apparent reason?

And does it happen a lot even when you know it shouldn't be happening? Or are you in a relationship where you don't know how to commit further and take it to the next level? And you always ask yourself: Why isn't my relationship moving forward?

Every time you think about this subject, do you want to avoid dealing with it because it makes you even more distant and withdrawn to the point where you fear your Queen might leave you? Are you feeling absolutely helpless and frustrated because you want to make her understand how much you want to be with her? You could be holding yourself back with past conditioning and making it impossible to relax and enjoy your new Female Led Relationship.

This is where *Love & Obey* affirmations can create a turning point and provide a real purpose. It is time to make service to your Queen a priority by changing your thinking and conditioning with these daily affirmations. I recognized a long time ago, after writing my second book *Real Men Worship Women*, that men need rules to follow in order to create the right relationship groundwork and to get through the transition.

If men understand these rules early on, then there will be less conflict, stress, and anxiety in the transition stage. This transition is the period when a man may desire change, but he must also change his way of thinking, which has been ingrained in him from youth. Properly worshipping the Queen requires reprogramming at the subconscious level, along with following all of the rules daily. When a man has achieved reprogramming, the woman is going to feel more confident and relaxed. Both you and your Queen can be relaxed. Once you have reprogrammed your patriarchal thinking, it will be easier to address the Queen as supreme.

Speech is important in Female Led Relationships. A man must obey his woman in his speech, calling her Goddess, Queen, or Mistress. "Yes, Queen, of course, my Goddess." "As you command, my Queen." By adding speech in the form of affirmations to worship her daily, you can change past conditioning. Female led will become as normal as brushing your teeth and flossing. The more ingrained a female led life is in men, the fewer disagreements and the more opportunity to create a deeper, more intimate connection.

You will repeat things like "I obey my Queen," "My life is to love, obey, and serve the Queen," and "I will honor and respect my Queen each and every day." Every great institution has an honor code—it's the extra layer of accountability. Turning point affirmations are like your honor code, and when you say use them with real intention, you create changes in yourself and your approach to female led life and your Queen.

The breakdown in relationships occurs when women and men are unsure of their roles, and this struggle can exist when couples focus overly on "equality" in a relationship. There is no equality in governments or organizations and rarely is it achieved in relationships. How often does anything get accomplished if everyone in the firm is equal and there is no leader? Usually never. The same is true in relationships. Women have allowed themselves to believe that the best they can hope for is equality. The pursuit of equality eventually leads to disagreement and power struggles.

At some point, one person needs to step up and take the lead. For years, the man was expected to take on that role, but today, in a Female Led Relationship, the Queen needs to take leadership in making the decisions and managing the day-to-day activities. There is a reason the saying, "Happy wife, happy life," exists. When the Queen is happy, you, as the supportive gentleman, will be happy too. The challenge occurs when a man must change his thinking on a deeper level. Perhaps you are just discovering female led life, but you have been conditioned to be patriarchal. Many men are raised by women, but having divorced parents tends to affect how men will view their position in relationships. Men may have a desire to submit, but desire and doing this daily with their Queens can be problematic. This is where reprogramming comes in and affirmations can be beneficial.

CHAPTER 35
Smash the Patriarchy

Many relationships begin to unravel when there is too much unhealthy conditioning happening, which is why it is necessary for you to smash the patriarchal conditioning in order for your Female Led Relationship to thrive. For example, you have been together with your partner for a while and have developed poor communication habits. With increasing arguments and disagreements, you both just ignore it.

Psychologist Patricia Evans discusses negative conditioning that occurs in relationships. She tells the story of a scientist who uses two frogs to study the effects of conditioning. The scientist places the first frog in a pan of hot water. The frog immediately jumps out. She places the second frog in a pan of cold water while the scientist gradually turns up the heat. The frog doesn't move. The scientist gradually turns up the heat again. The frog continues to stay. The scientist continues to turn up the heat, and yet again, the frog stays. Finally, the scientist turns up the heat to a boiling point. The frog continues to stay until it's boiled to death. This is similar to abuse, which often starts out slowly, and gradually picks up speed and intensity.

Unfortunately, this pattern can continue unending for years and years. Slowly, day by day, a person's soul gets chipped away. One day the person wakes up and realizes he/she has been sitting in a pan of boiling water. The reason conditioning is a powerful part of all relationships is that it can hinder progress, particularly when it is necessary to make major changes in having to create a Female Led Relationship. Affirmations and daily practice can go a long way to changing unhealthy conditioning, and for the Female Led Relationships, patriarchal conditioning.

Couple's therapist and bestselling author Terry Real is a member of the senior faculty at the Family Institute of Cambridge and Director of the Gender Relations program at the Meadows Institute in Arizona. Terry Real says, "We all live under patriarchy, which is a rigid dichotomy of gender roles. Traditionally, men are supposed to be strong and feel independent, unemotional, logical, and confident. Women are supposed to be expressive, nurturing, weak, and dependent. One of the things I say about those traditional gender roles is they don't make anybody happy, and they don't make for intimacy."

He believes that in order to lead men and women into happiness and intimacy, they must be led out of patriarchy since they are old rules not built for intimacy and happiness. He says, "The essence of masculinity is contempt for the feminine. Misogyny and masculinity are flip sides of the same coin. What it means to be a "man" today is not to be a girl. Not be feminine. Contempt for being feminine is part of the patriarchal culture." This leads to more unhealthy relationships, which could be part of the reason why the divorce rate is at 50 percent.

What's worse is that the real origin of patriarchy is not really known. Patriarchy is associated with a set of ideas — a patriarchal ideology that acts to explain and justify this dominance and attributes it to inherent natural differences between men and women. If we truly analyze what men want, patriarchy also fails to fulfill these needs. In a recent study, men described the reason leading to their divorces and what they most value in a woman. From this, it was concluded that the goal of men is to reduce complexity in their lives and what men want most from women is to feel truly appreciated. It's all about simplicity and appreciation.

Female Led Relationships address both of these needs. A strong woman in charge helps to simplify things because she leads while the man follows. In addition, when a man worships and serves a woman correctly, he will feel appreciated and rewarded. Female Led Relationships are growing because they are congruent with the state of our existence.

With women leading, there is much more emphasis on communication and empathy. The world needs more communication in a digital world and not much brute strength. A man can begin to develop his intuitive, empathetic side with affirmations that focus on serving his woman. Not only does this place focus on his woman daily, but he also retains a goal and purpose in his life.

CONCLUSION

The Female Led Relationship is one of the most exciting adventures you and your Queen will embark on. At the source of female led is obedience, discipline, and submission. Your role is to serve her, and she must lead. You each have a responsibility in the relationship to take care of your part while coming together and communicating with love and respect for each other. Rules and boundaries help with day-to-day life, but no matter what experience you decide to explore, there must always be consent.

Modern life means there needs to be a modern relationship, and the Female Led Relationship is timely with female empowerment and the Future is Female, so you can be confident that your union helps both of you to evolve. Female led life has the ability to transform your relationship or marriage, and couples have reported more intimacy and connection. There are many different experiences to explore together, including female led sex, oral pleasure, chastity, cuckolding, consensual non-monogamy, spanking, BDSM, and discipline.

One of the challenges for men is to release past patriarchal conditioning, but with the help of daily affirmations of female worship, you can overcome this, which helps you to learn to accept your Queen as your supreme leader and Goddess. It is my hope that you both will experience the transformative effects of female led life and the *Love & Obey* movement that thousands of couples have worldwide.

Printed in Great Britain
by Amazon

36449575R00136